TASTE IN MUSIC

Birch Tree
2am
In Degrees
Spanish Sahara
Red Sox
(Providence)
Mountain
================
Snake Oil
Inhaler
Two Steps. Twice

TASTE IN MUSIC

Eating on Tour with Indie Musicians

by ALEX BLEEKER & LUKE PYENSON

CHRONICLE BOOKS

SAN FRANCISCO

For Lauren and Leanne

Contents

HOW WAS TOUR?

All touring musicians know this question well, but depending on who's asking, it can be tricky to answer. Going On Tour has long been a heavily mythologized way of life, with ample touchpoints across pop culture. And yet, those who haven't gone on tour sometimes lack the context to fully appreciate what it actually means. We've gone off to play a single depressing college show in Pennsylvania, only to return home that same night and have someone ask, "How was tour?"

One show in Pennsylvania? That's not a tour. But tour's also not *Almost Famous*, at least not for everyone. In our little corner of the industry, indie rock, tour is many things—*too* many things, in fact, to sum up succinctly. And it's different for us all. Of course, tour represents the beautiful exchange between Band and Audience, the singular, ecstatic marvel of live music. But that lasts about an hour, sometimes two, rarely three. The rest of tour—the majority—is governed by two things: travel and food.

As indie musicians, we're both defined by and reliant on our relationship to movement. The amount of time we spend in the studio is absolutely dwarfed by the amount of time we spend on the road. And once we get on the road, the amount of time we spend onstage is dwarfed by the amount of time we spend in transit and at the table. With the advent of streaming services, most musicians don't make a living off their recorded music anymore; the bulk of our income comes from relentless cycles of touring that keep us in perpetual motion. During an average cycle, it's common to be on tour for about 150 nights out of the year.

And just as travel television hosts have local fixers schlepping them around from restaurant to restaurant, we, too, have a vast international network of colleagues, friends, and peers who show us where to eat or cook for us in their homes. And we don't want to sound flippant or ungrateful—but sometimes, musicians remember their meals more vividly than their shows.

•••

In May 2017, our bands Real Estate and Frankie Cosmos went on tour together around the Northeast and Midwest. We played some great shows—of course—but we also smuggled thick slices of rhubarb pie backstage from Tandem Coffee + Bakery in Portland, Maine; we detoured from Detroit to Dearborn for late-night Lebanese; we ordered deep-dish to the green room in Chicago. In short, we discovered we were each the resident food obsessive in our respective bands and forged a friendship centered around an appreciation of food, travel, and music, all of which have long been important to us both.

We'd taken separate but parallel paths to get where we were. After years spent on shoestring DIY tours, we both graduated to the comfortable-yet-modest confines of mid-level indie rock. Between tours, Luke spent time sharpening his food and recipe writing, while Alex took various front-of-house positions at one of his favorite Brooklyn restaurants. It made sense that we brought these passions on the road with us, finding both comfort and resonance in the universality of food no matter where we went. Eventually, luck intervened, and we ended up in the same place at the same time.

After that fateful first Real Estate–Frankie Cosmos tour, intertwining tour schedules brought us together for more memorable meals and moments—and that's not uncommon. The indie-rock universe is actually a pretty small world. Bands on the same well-worn circuit either know or are peripherally aware of one another. We play the same venues and festivals, follow the same routes from city to city, and work with the same promoters. For a field so global in scale, there's an astounding sense of community and interconnectedness.

All that ground to a halt during the Covid pandemic, which left the two of us sidelined from touring. Separated from our bands and the greater ecosystem of live music, we were each privately dealing with some introspection about our careers (e.g., Why did we do this at all? Will we ever do it again? What do we do now?).

Independently, we started to revisit a vague book idea we had thrown around before, albeit in slightly different forms. Alex was dreaming up a musicians' guide to eating on tour, full of off-the-beaten-track restaurant recommendations. Luke was seriously considering anthropology PhD programs where he could infuse his own music-industry experience into an academic study of touring musicians.

Before long, we were revisiting our ideas together—and then combining them. The book began to take shape organically as we tapped into our extensive networks and chatted with dozens of indie musicians representing several different subgenres, scenes, and eras. Apart from being fascinating and fun, each call felt like the best therapy session we'd ever had. We had to bottle that energy and share it.

We began collecting essays based broadly on the subject of eating on tour, and found that each story brought to mind different aspects of our own experiences moving through the world. Our suspicion—that food looms large in both the physical and emotional lives of touring musicians—was confirmed. And what's more, we found that stories centering food are the perfect gateway into understanding tour itself.

•••

Three-plus years have elapsed since we began working on this project—Real Estate put out a new album and started touring again, and Alex formed a subversive jam band called Taper's Choice. Frankie Cosmos put out a new album, Luke and his bandmate Lauren got married, and they amicably left the band after just a release show, their final tour thwarted by extenuating circumstances. The live-music industry, still in its pandemic slumber when our work here began, has more than bounced back. While there was always an archival bent to this book, the touring culture we've documented is very much alive today, even as our relationships to it evolve.

We've done our best to curate this collection like we'd curate a festival—making sure to include folks from different parts of the world, with different backgrounds, representing different generations. Within the following pages, there are artists from Mississippi, New Zealand, New Orleans, Uruguay, Algeria, Japan, Alaska, the UK, the Bronx, and more. We have a '70s art-pop icon, an '80s underground pioneer, an influential '90s rhythm section, early-aughts folk rockers, and current stars of the indie scene.

And alongside these musicians, we had to include a handful of the legendary promoters who take top care of touring artists, as well as the private chef who's sure to become the envy of every touring band. A couple of food writers make appearances in our Rest Stop featurettes, which focus on roadside dining culture in a few key locations around the world. But they aren't the only ones with clips—several contributing musicians are also published writers or poets. Several others are publishing pieces of writing here for the first time, though you'd never know.

We would have loved to include perspectives from front-of-house crews, tour managers, and the many others who make up the touring industry, but that'll have to wait for another volume. In fact, with such a vast subject, there are many things we weren't able to include. But here's what we do have.

In addition to wide-angle meditations about eating on tour, we've gathered stories that take place on five continents, in private homes, and at street-side stalls. In temples of fine dining and in actual temples. Backstage and in the van. Early in the morning and late at night.

Stories that deal with the best parts of touring: meaningful cultural exchange, hospitality-induced euphoria, and the opportunity to build relationships around the world.

And the worst parts of touring: loneliness, exhaustion, estrangement from family and friends, struggles with disordered eating, and unsteady access to medical care.

So the question isn't "How was tour?" It's "What do you eat on tour?" The conversations and essays that follow, like the best songs or meals, evoke something central about the human experience. They show us all the ways that music and food bring us together, break us down, lift us up, and add color to our lives.

Chapter One

It's Time for Tajik Breakfast: Hospitality in the Green Room and Beyond

It's a familiar still life. Set on a table in the green room, a bunch of bananas, a bowl of apples, a loaf of sliced bread, a meat-and-cheese tray, a bowl of mixed nuts, a flat of bottled water, and hummus. Always, no matter what, hummus. This tablescape, either more austere or more lavish depending on the band and the venue, is what often constitutes *hospitality* for touring indie bands—in industry jargon, that's the term we use. And of the many words that pass the lips and occupy the minds of musicians on tour, there is perhaps none more important.

Hospitality—in our world—refers not only to the idea of host-guest relations and the rituals that govern them, but also literally to the bowl of apples, the bunch of bananas, the meat-and-cheese tray, and the hummus. The word is used in countless ways, countless times per day, and in almost every case, *hospitality* either implies or directly involves food.

Venues and promoters have a *hospitality budget* for each show, which goes toward satisfying a band's *hospitality rider*. The food items off that rider procured with that budget comprise part or all of that evening's *hospitality*. In some cases, especially at festivals, an emissary reveals themself to be *in charge of hospitality for you guys* and might direct you to the *hospitality tent*, where the food is. You might finish soundchecking, when somebody peeks their head into your green room to *take care of hospitality* and hands you an envelope of cash (buyouts) or a stack of meal vouchers. Alternatively, you might search tirelessly around the venue for somebody in charge, only to be told that there is *no hospitality* or that it's one drink ticket per member.

In the late 1950s, the anthropologist A. M. Hocart wrote on "the divinity of the guest" in his book *The Life-Giving Myth and Other Essays*. This is a concept well known to many societies, and in the Western tradition it can be traced to Homeric times. In ancient Greece, all travelers were thought to be accompanied by gods and thus deserving of equal treatment. In some cases, travelers actually *were* gods, testing the moral fiber of ordinary folks by passing through their towns in disguise and accepting whatever hospitality was offered.

I like to imagine Zeus backstage, contemplating a half-eaten tub of hummus and rubbing a single drink ticket between his fingers. There's a knock at the door. "Hey, man, I've got buyouts . . ."

Of course, hospitality extends beyond the biome of the show itself and out into the real world too. Because while our experiences on tour generally revolve around the show and its attendant cast of characters, we do occasionally get a night, or at least a few hours, off. Some of the most memorable moments on tour can be traced back to being hosted and fed—by friends, by family, by friends' family, family friends, perfect strangers, colleagues, and others both easily categorized and not.

On the nights that we're treated like Greek deities and everything clicks into place, there's nothing better. When things go the other way, well . . . at least we get a good story. These experiences have an indelible effect on our moods, our relationships to one another, and ultimately even the performances we put on for each audience.

A couple of years ago in the northwestern Spanish city of A Coruña, I was treated to a multicourse, wine-fueled banquet of Galician specialties with my father-in-law's friend's friends. Normally, a regional feast alongside random European septuagenarians is quite literally a dream come true, but I was there in my capacity as the drummer of a mid-level indie band, not as an insatiable food adventurer.

The table was filled with pulpo a la gallega, sardine empanadillas, and fried artichokes; our hosts ensured my wine glass remained perpetually full no matter how much I drank. When I thought the meal was winding down, a local breed of pork was trotted out, and my wine glass was of course refilled. Everything about the meal—the setting, the food, the company—was perfect, except that it immediately preceded an hour-long set of live music.

I had to excuse myself from the table to speed-walk the twenty minutes back to the venue, where I had only a moment to compose myself before taking the stage. It's great, on nights like this, that we drummers get to sit down. But that night, sitting down felt like standing up, and standing up felt like passing away. I could not tell you a single thing about the performance.

Examples of similar nights and many other permutations of on-the-road hospitality follow in the chapter ahead. We'll hear from Devendra Banhart and Andy Cabic on Japanese pre-show-meal etiquette, and Kevin Morby on Thanksgiving dinner in Portugal. Sasami Ashworth will share memories of staying with a Guinness heir in Ireland, and Auckland's The Beths fondly recall post-show pancakes at their sound engineer's parents' house in suburban Ohio. If you're from New Zealand, that's a pretty exotic proposition!

We'll also hear from Hand Habits' Meg Duffy about a tension-filled tasting menu at Iceland Airwaves, and from the James Beard–nominated chef (and noted rocker) Cheetie Kumar on the roots of her beloved Raleigh restaurant Garland and its upstairs music venue, Kings. Plus, thanks to drummer Chris Frantz, we get to drop in on Talking Heads' majestic first meal in Paris alongside the Ramones. Most would agree that's an example of veritable gods passing through town—and even gods need to eat. *-LP*

They're Feeding You Tonight

Devendra Banhart in conversation with Andy Cabic (Vetiver)

One of the most surreal and delightful aspects of a career in music is the rare opportunity to meet some of your heroes. I had been listening to Devendra Banhart and Andy Cabic for years before I got to know either of them socially. Fans of theirs will be happy to know that they are both kind and charismatic gentlemen. I was hosting Andy for dinner over at my place one night when he told me a wild tale about a feast he'd eaten at a temple after a show in Kanazawa, Japan. Naturally I was like, "Wait, can you tell that story again?"

Andy suggested that he and Devendra could tell the story together from memory, so we got them on the phone with each other to do just that. It was a serious delight to be a fly on the wall for the following conversation. These two veterans of the road really nailed all the fine points (both high and low) of eating on tour and far away from home. –AB

Photo by Alissa Anderson.

Devendra Banhart: You're hungry all the time on tour. But you don't wanna get too filled up before playing a show; at least that's my experience. And then the show's over, and it's like midnight, and where are you gonna eat?

Tour is like, how am I gonna figure out how to get a good meal at these weird hours, and tour is survival mode in so many ways. And it's such a privilege to be able to be on tour, it's such a luxury, that you can only kind of talk about tour with other people who have toured. Because if not, you sound like a total ungrateful asshole, you know, as opposed to just an asshole.

Andy Cabic: Well, the story—I wish I could go back to that meal! I wish I could do that meal over again; I wish I could savor and remember each thing that was on the table.

DB: I think that's quite potent—Andy doesn't want to go back on tour; he wants to go back to that meal.

AC: My memory is that we had a whirlwind tour of Japan, and we were in a different city pretty much every day. This was maybe the most special of them all because it was at a temple; I think it's called Kouseiji.

We were hungry; I mean, Devendra, I remember in particular, was hungry. Our tour manager, this guy Kozuki Tomita—Kozuki was very sweet and would always talk with us in very hushed tones, with his hand over his mouth—he's like, "They're feeding you tonight," and Devendra was like, "That's great, that's amazing, but I'm a little hungry now, and the show's a couple of hours away. Can we just stop somewhere and get some food and see the town?"

DB: I need to interject: Andy is trying to illustrate that perhaps our tour manager was so polite that while he *knew* what was in store, because of my insistence, he relented. I think just mentioning that there would be food later that night was his version of making it very clear that there was a big surprise in store. But, of course, I'm a stupid American and I'm like, "Nah, nah, I gotta eat!"

AC: He's totally right; that's how Kozuki was. He was being so polite!

DB: The only reason I'm so stressed about eating is that not only am I trying to eat in time to digest by the time we play, but I'm also in my favorite city, my favorite *country* in the

world, with my favorite *cuisine* in the world! Andy too! We're so excited, we love to eat, and the adventure of finding a good restaurant, especially on tour—it's wonderful.

AC: So we found this sushi-boat place, which, in the whole time we were there, we had not eaten at a place like that. I think there was something kitschy about going to a sushi-boat place.

DB: Just to make it clear, we're not going to Yoshinoya [a Japanese fast-food chain] while we're in Japan, but the sushi boat was the closest thing to something a little bit novel that we could find at that moment. I got a little funny kick of eating this corny sushi boat while I was in Japan, but it was still really tasty.

I did this silly thing, which was to just eat anywhere, because everywhere in Japan is so good anyways. Because after the show I'm expecting four grains of rice and a little bit of tea, which is fine. I'm happy to eat that; what an honor to play at a temple. This is where I'm at. "Hey, Devendra, be humble, and be grateful you got to play this beautiful temple, and just drop your expectations; this is monastic food, a monastic environment."

AC: And then we played the show. We've done a few tours like this; we're onstage at the same time, and we pretty much go back and forth. We do one or two songs of mine, or two of his, some covers, acoustic or electric. These were very intimate shows, and that was really remarkable. The people, just two feet away from you, just big smiles on their faces, both of us not believing we're there. The surroundings were so beautiful.

We took a moment afterward, and then we went into their kitchen and sat down around this table, probably seven feet long—surrounded by the people who lived at the temple—which was just filled with food. And every time a dish was finished, another one was put down in its place. This went on for a few hours, and I remember within, like, the first like ten minutes looking at Dev and our eyes meeting like, "Oh. This is a serious meal here that they're doing for us."

DB: It was this incredible spread—there was uni, there was soba, there was ramen, there were these beautiful blocks of

Opposite: Andy (left) and Devendra (right) in Devendra's kitchen in LA.
Photo by Alissa Anderson.

tofu, so much fish, and shirako, which is one of my favorite things in the world, beautiful cod sperm just, like, melting! Just gorgeous cod sperm. And natto, which is another of my favorite foods in the world, *abounds*, and bottles of sake that just reach the fucking ceiling! I fucked it up by eating sushi boat, but it was still so incredible, we stuffed ourselves.

Right now as we're talking about this, I'm thinking about our experiences of promoters feeding us after a show, and that is such an Asian thing, it's a European thing, it's an African thing, but it's *not* an American thing. Maybe at the DIY level you're gonna get fed, but generally speaking the idea that a promoter's gonna feed you after a show in the United States? Are you *fucking* kidding me? No fucking way!

Generally you go to a show, and you see the band, and they play their nice show, and maybe that night was a date night, and you went and you had a nice meal with your partner, and you dressed up nice and then you went to the show, and you saw the band play, and that was nice; they played nice. But that band has not *eaten*, not *slept*, not taken a *shit*, not like, it's like they're—they're in hell! They've been in hell.

That's why it's such a rare thing to have had this incredible feast. At a temple nonetheless! That night in Kanazawa, we were being wined and dined; we were guests of honor. The generosity, the elegance and grace of that generosity, was just permeating that space, and we felt like the belles of the ball. I mean, we felt really cared for and loved, and that is the rarest thing on tour.

Man is that rare.

Opposite: Photo by Alissa Anderson.

Thanksgiving in Porto

by Kevin Morby

Tour dates have to be mutually agreed upon by quite a large number of people. Agents, promoters, record labels, artists, and crew are all involved in the decision-making process, and often this process pays little attention to birthdays, wedding anniversaries, holidays, and other significant events. We meet the Kansas City–based troubadour Kevin Morby in Portugal during one such significant event, the 2016 US presidential election.

Kevin Morby is well loved in our corner of the music world, and I'm not just talking about his adoring fans—musicians love him too. Before he was a prolific indie-folk songwriter, Kevin and I came up together in the north Brooklyn indie-rock scene and became friends when he played bass in the band Woods. We'd spend long summer days together talking about the peculiarities of our chosen musical lives. I always admired his insight, and for that reason he was the first person I asked to contribute to this collection. You'll understand why. *-AB*

There is a lot that I don't remember about eating on the road. And though I've been given the good fortune to dine all over the world over the past decade, I'd be hard-pressed to tell you the actual names of most of the restaurants, neighborhoods, or even the cities and towns in which the dining took place. These names, like the names of most people I've met and venues and hotels I've been in over the past twelve years, tend to escape me. Instead of trying to relocate them, I simply let them settle quietly into my past not as a specific time, place, or person, but rather as a *feeling*.

For example: I remember *feeling cool* as I ate sushi in Tokyo at sunrise. I remember *feeling cozy* while eating pierogi in a cabin in Poland. And I remember *feeling fancy* while eating smoked fish at an Icelandic spa. But could I guide you to exactly where these experiences took place? Probably not. Trying to recall the details of a tour—much less where I ate while on that tour—for me, is like trying to recall the details of a dream. Its beauty is in the mystery and the absurd—in the not making sense. And to make sense of, or locate, the exact details would simply rob these magic memories of their warmth.

These warm magical memories, though, of course live next to and are usually greatly outnumbered by the many cold and dark moments of dining that touring in an indie-rock band is much more likely to present you with. Believe you me, it is not all sushi at sunrise and smoked fish in Icelandic spas. I could tell you, if you dared to ask, about the thousands—literally, probably thousands!—of sad, soggy gas-station sandwiches I've pushed into my mouth, or the dozens of Chili's Too airport burgers I've forced down my throat. About the food poisoning that will go out of its way to find you out there on the road or about the post-gig Taco Bell and the hungover Egg McMuffin that follows the next morning. I could even tell you about my first tours, when we would dumpster-dive for bagels, pizza, and expired produce from health-food stores across America.

I could, but I won't! Instead, here is a list, off the top of my head, of some things I know for certain about food on tour:

- Swedish gas stations are actually just candy stores.

- Japanese 7-Elevens are cleaner and have better food than most restaurants in America.

- Australia takes breakfast *very* seriously.

- There is a waitstaff at most McDonald's in Scandinavia.

- Poutine is only in Montreal; don't go asking for it in Toronto.

- In the American South I get excited about two things: Bojangles and Cook Out.

- Actually, make that three things: boiled peanuts inside most every gas station when below the Mason-Dixon Line east of the Mississippi.

- The Pacific Northwest is a wonderland of great Vietnamese food.

- You should never eat a doughnut at a Tim Hortons while in Canada . . .

- . . . but eventually, you will eat a doughnut at a Tim Hortons!

And the list, I'm afraid, full of this kind of information, could go on forever. Little useless tidbits that I've retained over the years, usually centered around roadside fast food, convenience stores, and gas stations. A meal on tour, after all, is a shift meal. Something not really meant to be enjoyed, but rather to fuel the process of sitting around for fourteen hours a day and performing for two.

But if you make the time, be it a quick soundcheck, day off, or a pre- or post-tour vacation, you can find the good stuff too. I often have, usually guided by the hand of someone who knows the area. And I know what you must be thinking: Do I really not remember the names of any of *those* restaurants? The honest answer is okay, fine, I do, and one in particular stands out: Tapabento, right in the heart of Porto, my favorite city in all of Europe. The vibe is impeccable, but unfortunately—and sometimes this is the case with the best restaurants—I cannot recommend what to order. It's just not that kind of place. Just let the night guide you, and ask the staff what they recommend.

Not far from Tapabento, though, just outside of Porto, in the seaside town of Espinho, is the site of my favorite tour-food memory. It was at the tail end of one of the longest and most depressing tours I'd ever been on. It also happened to be Thanksgiving. And despite the shows being well attended, that specific tour had the long, dark shadow of our forty-fifth president-elect cast all over it.

Our kickoff show had been four weeks earlier, on election night, and while it was meant to be a night of celebration, not only of our sold-out show in London and the tour ahead, but also for the election of the first female president of the United States, we all know what happened instead. What followed, for us, was a long, cold, and wet month on the road through mainland Europe.

By the time we arrived in Portugal, we had only two shows left, and though our spirits were broken, I was happy to see a familiar face in our friend André Gomes, who was promoting our show that night. André had to remind us that it was Thanksgiving back home in America, as we had forgotten about the holiday, which stood as a testament to our feelings toward our home at that time— somewhere confusingly between *homesick* and *sick at the thought of home*. And while our friends and families were surely coming together to discuss and argue over the current state of affairs, we were headed to a restaurant next door to the theater where André had made us a reservation.

As an American traveling through Europe, there is this sense that you're inside the movie of your life in real time while simultaneously watching it through the lens of an older version of yourself up on the big screen. In the movie of my life, the scene where I walked into that restaurant is pivotal.

Inside, we were seated at a long, candlelit table set with large carafes of water and wine. The whole touring party was there, and the evening, despite everything, somehow felt festive. André ordered for the table and explained that the menu was small and consisted of only meat, fish, potatoes, and salad but insisted we try and share it all. He explained that all the food was cooked inside a large wood-burning stove to which the whole restaurant was anchored.

Our meals came out staggered as we shared among ourselves, and the food was exactly perfect: comforting and soulful. From there, though we had a show to play, the night seemed to go on for hours as a tangible warmth—one that we had lacked for weeks—encompassed us all. Remembering that evening, and that meal, now is like trying to recall a dream inside a dream. To this day, I don't know the name of the restaurant, or exactly what I ate, or what year the wine was from. But I do know that, at one point, the power in the restaurant went out, and suddenly there was no light save the warm glow of the fire from the wood-burning stove illuminating all our faces, smiles and all.

There is a lot I don't remember about eating on the road, but I do remember that.

Kevin in Madrid. Photo by Alex Bleeker.

Farls at Pickering Forest

by Sasami Ashworth (SASAMI)

Plenty of nights on tour are spent in accommodations that range from modest to horrid to just downright weird. I once spent the night sleeping on the living room floor of a friend's friend's parents' house in Ohio because they were hoarders. There were several spare bedrooms, but all the surfaces were spoken for.

Occasionally, however, circumstance will place you in some sort of unexpectedly awe-inspiring location, as it did Sasami Ashworth—who performs as SASAMI—one night in Ireland. Some of the best friends I've made from touring are a part of Dublin's thriving indie scene, and Ireland is near to my heart. So when Sasami mentioned staying at an incredible country manor outside Dublin, she lit up, and so did I. I knew exactly which manor she was talking about. *–LP*

I studied classical French horn from middle school through college and, until my mid-twenties, the only "tour" I'd ever done was a short Italian run around the Umbria Jazz Festival. This was before becoming a full-time, hardcore, rock-and-rolling road dog; I was playing in a jazz ensemble. Once I joined the rock world, my late twenties were characterized by hundreds of nights spent in hotel beds and shits taken in gas-station bathrooms (the less-glamorous sides of going on tour). But I keep thinking of another early tour experience that took place in Europe, before all of that.

Several years ago, I was enlisted by Harper Simon (son of Paul) to rearrange his rock record for a whimsical orchestration of horn, a couple of strings, bass clarinet, and Harper on guitar. We were also going to do a short stint performing the songs across Europe. Our first show was in Dublin, and all I knew was that we were staying with friends of Harper's in Celbridge, County Kildare, a little west of the city.

We pulled up to a three-story, stony Georgian country-castle, and I was immediately enchanted both by the heavenly bucolic setting and by the parade of creatures we met along the mile-long driveway. There were four dogs (Cerberus, Ragga, Fidget, and Daisy), four horses (Rory, Blue, Death Trap, and Supermac's), and a gaggle of local kids with instruments roaming in and out ad libitum. Finally, we were greeted by the blue-eyed matriarch of the operation, Marina Guinness. Yes, much to my surprise, we were crashing with one of Ireland's very own Guinness heirs. And this, I learned, was Pickering Forest House.

We dropped our bags in the foyer and made our way through the house, encountering along the way a table of thirty or so half-empty booze bottles (seemingly decades old), a couple of Greek white-marble busts, and a complete suit of plate armor with a taxidermied cat head casually peeking out of the helmet. At the heart of the house was Marina's kitchen and its quintessential cast-iron farmhouse stove, which both heats the house and provides sustenance to its inhabitants and guests. Naturally, this is the room where all the fun happens.

In this exquisite manor house, with its verdant grandeur and impressive lineage, all illusions of a romantically royal existence were immediately extinguished at that first sight of a scraggly-haired Marina smoking a cigarette while flipping bacon ("rashers," they call 'em) in that glorious kitchen. She may be the direct descendant of illustrious brewery fame, but her vibe couldn't be less pretentious or highfalutin. If Marina is the duchess of anything, it is of freaks, wayfarers, renegades, and regular people.

Something of a legend in the Irish music scene, Marina is one of those people who knows *everyone*, and whom everyone knows. Mention her name to an Irish musician, or almost any rock or pop musician who's passed through Ireland, and there'll be a smile of recognition. One of Marina's claims to fame is that, for many years, she's opened her family home to musicians in need of a practice space. Which is how I found myself there.

But back to the food. Because despite the décor that felt like a cross between a nineteenth-century oddball museum and some sort of fairy-tale frat house, the most memorable part of my first stay at Pickering Forest House was the food (and the mirth, a close second). Irish soda bread with jam and the best local butter you've ever had, rashers of thick-cut Irish bacon, orange-yolked farm-fresh eggs, grilled tomatoes, and the most magical breakfast eatable: potato farls. Potato farls, potato fadge, potato cakes, griddle cakes, boxty, whatever you want to call them—fry 'em up, fill me up, and put me in the ground—they are *that* good. Often made with leftover mashed potatoes, potato farls are like perfect chewy, fluffy griddle cakes or fry bread. Or like giant, flat gnocchi fried in bacon grease. Mmmmmm!

The aforementioned soda bread is an equally bodacious Irish carb option. It is denser than American bread and features baking soda (called bicarbonate of soda in Ireland) as the rising agent, which makes it quicker and easier to prepare than yeasted breads. I don't know if it's the psychology of getting beyond my emaciated hometown of Los Angeles or if European breads are actually different on a cellular level, but the loaves over there just *feel* better!

The best part of all of this is that Marina and her "kids" (they are now in their thirties), Violet and Finbar, kept me all keyed up and laughing on Irish tea and unbelievable personal tales of questionable veracity (Violet's words, not mine). That's the mirth I mentioned before.

I have now stayed at Pickering Forest House many times over the years, and I'm pretty sure I've had breakfast for every meal, morning or night. Washed down, of course, with a Guinness.

Opposite: Outside Pickering Forest House. Photo by Luke Pyenson.

The kitchen and a living area at Pickering Forest House. Photos by Luke Pyenson.

Masa-san and the Box of Hoshigaki

by Luke Pyenson

The ritual of giving and receiving gifts is central to hospitality around the world, and touring musicians can be on both sides of the equation. Usually we're giving folks vinyl or T-shirts, but in Frankie Cosmos we always strove to pick up a bottle of wine or a dozen bagels for the people who graciously hosted us early on.

I've been given many things on tour—fresh grapefruits from my friend Jason's parents' backyard in Phoenix, a Ziploc bag full of homemade cinnamon buns from my mother-in-law's friend in Stockholm, and bean-to-bar chocolate featuring green mango from a Frankie Cosmos fan who'd traveled from Manila to Jakarta to see us play. All of these left an impression.

I could've written about any of them, actually, but one gift stands out among the rest. And I don't even know the person who gave it to me. *-LP*

The mood was jubilant in the green room after our first show in Tokyo. Our local fixers, the promoters, the opening band, and a couple of local friends were coming in and out in the usual backstage post-show hubbub. But out of this hubbub, on this night, emerged a recognizable yet puzzling presence—a black-suited Japanese salaryman, bearing a gift. For me.

The man bowed his head wordlessly and offered me a shopping bag containing an enormous box, which freed him up to then present his business card with two outstretched hands. Next to his name, I read the familiar name of a cybersecurity firm that, at the time, also employed my father. Slowly I started to put the pieces together. I vaguely heard my dad's voice—months ago—telling me he'd mentioned our show to a Japanese colleague whom he had never met. That must be Masa-san.

I thanked him so much for coming, and for the gift, and he nodded, bowing. There was barely time for a selfie before he quickly left.

The box Masa gave me was, first of all, quite heavy. So I set it down on a table and called over my college friend Catherine—who had relocated to Tokyo after graduation—for the unboxing. Much to my wonderment, the box contained roughly two dozen individually (and impeccably) wrapped hoshigaki—dried Hachiya persimmons, no doubt of the absolute highest quality, the most pristine-looking, perfect, plump specimens imaginable. Catherine estimated that this offering would have set Masa-san back upward of one hundred dollars. I unwrapped one and took a bite.

My personal history with Hachiya persimmons began in November 2013, when I visited the farm in northern Italy where I'd volunteered a handful of summers before. Different things were in season this time, and the property's persimmon tree—*cachi* in Italian, from the Japanese *kaki*—was heavy with oblong Hachiyas. I was given one to taste, my first ever, and my mouth puckered immediately, overtaken first by a dizzying astringency, and then an all-consuming dryness. I thought of the French phrase *gueule de bois*, colloquially a hangover, but literally "wooden mouth." That's what I had. A Hachiya hangover.

A few years later, my wife reintroduced me to persimmons via the gentler Fuyu variety. Whereas Hachiyas are long and tapered, Fuyus are squat and tomato-like. Their deep-orange flesh, when unripe, slices like an apple and has a crisp bite and subtle sweetness. When ripe, the flesh begins to give slightly, and the flavor blossoms into sweet carrot with a hint of brown sugar. I couldn't believe this was the same fruit I had tried in Italy. I later learned that Hachiyas, when unripe, are so tannic as to be essentially inedible, and that my reaction was hardly uncommon. Had I waited till the skin was mottled and the flesh soft, I would have tasted the same sweet and floral depth I now associated with Fuyus.

And so, speaking of that sweet, floral depth—I don't need to tell you, I think, that this is just what washed over me as I enjoyed my first bite of hoshigaki in the green room of Basement Bar in Shimokitazawa. But dried versus fresh persimmon meant the sweetness was intense and jammy, and the texture can only, or ought to only, be described as mochi mochi—pleasantly chewy.

These days, the painstaking steps involved in producing top-quality hoshigaki are common knowledge to any self-respecting Food Person, but at the time (2017), I was not aware that these delicate fruits were individually strung up to dry for a period of several weeks and regularly hand massaged to encourage sugar development and guarantee that trademark texture. I knew they did this to the cows, for Kobe beef, but *persimmons*? No wonder they're such a treasured item in Japan—perfect for a gift.

Now, one of the interesting things about receiving gifts on tour is that, because space—physical space—is of such high value to touring musicians, gifts are sometimes thought of as—and I really hate to say this—a burden. And yet, people love to give us stuff. Young musicians give us burned CDs of their material, friendly fans bring us jars of homemade jam or goodies from the coffee shops they work at during the day, and local friends and family give us whatever they'd give us if we were visiting normally, not on tour. Thoughtful, lovely items that we almost assuredly do not have space for.

On domestic tours, this presents its own set of challenges, but on international tours, when every bit of luggage space needs to be economized to the absolute highest degree (lest we incur baggage fees or worse), it's a different ball game. I don't want to say that acquiring items on tour is totally off-limits, just that you have to have a plan. And for me, that plan often involved the some-what bottomless depths of my cymbal bag, the repository for everything that came into my possession on tour. This system finally met its match in Tokyo with the dozens of highest-quality dried persimmons conferred upon me by Masa-san: They just didn't all fit. I gave Catherine half and padded my cymbals with the rest.

One of the limits of my cymbal-bag system was that sometimes, unfortunately, items placed there for safekeeping did get lost in the shuffle. Packing and repacking my cymbals, wrapping them with Bubble Wrap, loading and unloading the T-shirts I use to dampen my drums, the sticks and other miscellany I keep in there—it was a lot to keep track of. And so that's how, about a year after our show in Tokyo, I found a cache of smooshed dried persimmons at the very bottom of my cymbal bag, a location not at all befitting such esteemed delicacies.

I did not feel good about this. I thought about the highly specific sequence of events that had taken place to bring Masa to Basement Bar that night a year before. A middle-aged salaryman in a sea of young Japanese hipsters, in a society highly stratified by personal appearance and adherence to subculture (or not), surely Masa would have felt a little out of place. But the act of my dad simply *mentioning* in an email that his son would be performing in Tokyo with his band could be taken as nothing less than an assignment. A mission. An imperative.

For months, Masa had this date marked off on his calendar to come to Shimokitazawa. He came, possibly from Aoyama or from Roppongi, on a packed subway car, and he had to suffer through an hour of introspective K Records–accented indie pop (possibly even through our two local openers that night) to ensure he'd catch me for the two-minute handoff of a gift worthy of a visiting American colleague, or the next best thing, his son.

I imagined Masa darting through the streets of Tokyo with the (again, *heavy*) box of persimmons. Maybe resting it carefully at his feet as he enjoyed a piece of grilled mackerel and some rice at an izakaya, or as he slurped a bowl of quick-serve ramen at a booth, or chomped a few skewers of yakitori at a street-side stall on his way to the gig. Maybe he received a call at one point and had to shift the box to one arm as he fumbled in his pocket for his phone. By the way, he also had a briefcase!

He did all of this—and I just want to emphasize, he couldn't have *possibly* enjoyed the show. I just won't accept that he could have enjoyed the show; he did not. He, like I said, suffered through this show, dreadfully uncomfortable in his suit (how could he not have been!), all the while protecting this absolutely precious cargo, a box of exquisite dried persimmons. A seasonal delight, a piece of cultural heritage, a synecdoche, in that moment, in this context, for no less than the entire country of Japan.

He waded through the audience, found his way to the green room, to me, bowed his head, and completed the mission. Such are the lengths to which, I learned, Japanese hosts are willing to go to make their guests not only feel special, but feel *welcome*, far from home.

I can't even imagine what he would have done for my dad.

Kings, Garland, and Beyond

as told by Cheetie Kumar
(the Cherry Valence; Birds of Avalon)

Co-owner of Kings (Raleigh) and Chef-Owner of Ajja (Raleigh)

On one of my early tours with Frankie Cosmos, I was fortunate to pass through Raleigh, North Carolina, to play at the rock club Kings. I was even more fortunate to eat at its downstairs restaurant, Garland. At the time, I didn't realize that both were co-owned by chef and musician Cheetie Kumar, a singular force in both the food and music worlds. And this being an early tour, I also didn't realize just how unique it was—especially in the US—to have a great restaurant attached to a great venue.

Cheetie isn't merely a chef who messes around with a guitar in her spare time. Her bands—first the Cherry Valence and then Birds of Avalon—are well-known stalwarts of the Triangle rock scene and have toured extensively around the US and Europe. Before opening the restaurant that would earn her multiple James Beard nominations, Cheetie was cobbling together meals in the back of the van for her extremely lucky bandmates. In a series of conversations with her, we learned that the hospitality blueprint for Kings and Garland was hatched—where else?—on tour.

At the time of writing, Cheetie had recently made the difficult decision to close Garland and open a new restaurant, Ajja, a couple of miles away. It may not have a venue above it, but Cheetie's remarkable story is alive in everything she does; I can't wait to eat there. –LP

Before I was a chef or a musician, I was a band manager. I did promotions at my college radio station and didn't want to move to New York or LA after graduation, so I just moved to Raleigh. I had a couple of friends here, and I really liked how it felt—my rent was cheap, and I got to figure out what I wanted to do. I was thinking, "Is there a world where there are cool managers that actually care for their bands?" So I did that right out of college, in the late '90s.

I was also working as the World's Worst Server at a restaurant: My first day, I dropped hot fries on somebody's head. Cool. My bands all got record deals, but then they broke up. I didn't know what I was gonna do, although I had just started playing guitar. My now-husband was like, "Well, that's what you really wanna do—you should just play!" Around the same time, I took my first restaurant kitchen job, but it was nothing fancy. It was like a sandwich shop.

Before long, I'd formed a band and we booked a tour, like you used to be able to just do in those days. On the road, I was always starving! The band's van was actually an ex–prison transport van, a Ford Econoline 350, and we built the loft like everybody did, but we didn't have back seats. I built and upholstered a bench with storage underneath. I kept a bin full of spices, hot sauce, peanut butter, and basically all the "hacks" I'd need to be able to cook at people's houses, hotel rooms, or campsites. I don't really watch *Chopped*, but I imagine it was like that: What can I make out of what's available for under ten dollars to feed seven people?

We had a cooler that was, like, our ottoman, and I forced us to go to grocery stores so we'd always have supplies. In desperate times, like in the middle of Montana or New Mexico late at night, we'd go to Subway and order salads without dressing, so we'd at least have vegetables. We had a George Foreman grill, we had a hot plate, and I'd be reading cookbooks and food magazines. The whole time I was touring, I'd be dreaming about food. And when I was home, I'd be cooking and dreaming about going on tour.

My first band, the Cherry Valence, was the first band to get to tour in Europe. I think we played in London first, and then we flew to Spain, and I remember thinking, "Oh my god, we're getting to do this?" It was amazing, and Spain really kind of changed everything. First of all, playing in Spain is just awesome. They love rock and roll, and we were a rock-and-roll band; our very first show we had to repeat songs because they wouldn't let us get offstage!

Our first shows were in Sant Feliu de Guíxols (north of Barcelona) and Madrid. I was trying to be vegetarian, so all I did was eat Spanish tortilla every day. But then we went to the Basque Country, and it was like the clouds parted and the angels sang. There were vegetable dishes and all these beautiful pintxos, just full of flavor and cheap! I remember fifteen restaurants in a row, and they were all producing these very thoughtful bites that were all perfect. Not only would the promoters take us out to dinner, but we would have a *nice* dinner. Nothing was off-limits, and they really treated us like humans.

In Spain, things just felt different. The clubs were a part of the community, and they were run by young people. It was clear that the arts and food scenes were all one big, important part of everyday life. It was such a refreshing vibe, and hugely inspiring. It made us wanna play better! We felt good about what we were doing, it gave us confidence, and we felt seen. It made me want to bring a kernel of that hospitality into anything we did, and it really fueled our drive to combine food and music.

Between tours, I'd transitioned to bartending because I made so much more money than in the kitchen. But I started doing a little bit of catering on the side and took on jobs that I really wasn't prepared to do. I also sometimes cooked for bands when they played at Kings, but this was the old Kings—in a different location and without a restaurant underneath. My husband was a partner; I wasn't involved yet. Still, I remember cooking for Sharon Jones & the Dap-Kings when they came through. It was a Sunday, and I wanted to give them Sunday dinner, so I made smothered chicken.

Eventually, after my second band, Birds of Avalon, started to slow down touring, we had the opportunity to reopen Kings in a new location. The venue came first, and a few years later we opened Garland downstairs. Hospitality became a lot easier with Garland; if I got a band's rider in time, I could make them fresh hummus, for example, and it'd be warm and perfectly pureed. Just a little bit of thoughtfulness goes such a long way when you're not gonna be home for weeks at a time.

I feel like I could do an anthropological study on what different kinds of bands want to eat. I can predict what the rider is gonna be just from hearing their music. For a metal band, I'm not gonna cook for them; they don't care. They'd rather have their bottle of Crown Royal and fast food, so I'm not gonna worry about it. But an indie-rock band from Brooklyn, they're probably gonna be very health conscious. So let's make sure that they stay regular.

Some of the bigger bands we toured with have come into the restaurant to eat a couple of times. Like the Flaming Lips. For them it was like, "Oh my god! I can't believe you're doing this!" Same thing with the Raconteurs. We toured with them, and then they came here like, "How the fuck did you learn to cook?"

Going from saying "I'm going to open a restaurant" to becoming a chef is a pretty profound evolution and not something I expected at all. It's an eighty-seat restaurant with a nice bar; I wasn't gonna put sandwiches and quesadillas on the menu. When you're learning how to play your instrument, you learn your basics. You learn your rudimentary things like scales, or patterns if you're a drummer. Your fundamentals. And then that becomes a part of your vocabulary. The things I used to cook in the van on tour, or in the hotel room, or at somebody's house—it was better than what we could get otherwise, but it wasn't anything that I would put on a restaurant menu. But I learned how to do more with less.

I grew up in India until I was eight and a half years old, but I didn't want Garland to be an Indian restaurant. Most of my life has been in the US; I've seen this whole country, and I've seen a lot of Europe. I wanted to be able to make food about movement and migration. I really love the similarities of spices from region to region, and from country to country; I feel like it's an exercise in history and storytelling.

This project has taken a lot of my energy—my life force—but it has also provided me with a lot of satisfaction and fulfillment. A lot of times diners at Garland would say, "I've never had this before, but something about it makes me think of my grandmother." That's amazing, right? It's like a good song. You feel like you've heard it your whole life. You already know it.

Eating with Ghosts

by Damon Krukowski and Naomi Yang (Galaxie 500; Damon & Naomi)

When I was growing up as an indie kid in Greater Boston, local legends Damon Krukowski and Naomi Yang were always more important to me than, say, Aerosmith or the Dropkick Murphys. Their influence can be felt across a number of indie subgenres that they pioneered (dreampop, slowcore, psych-folk), and their creative practice remains robust to this day, in music as well as in writing, filmmaking, and more.

When we talked to Damon and Naomi about contributing to this book, they kept returning to one subject: Japan. This was true for many of the artists we spoke to, but Damon and Naomi have a particularly poignant relationship to this country, its underground rock scenes, its food, and its history.

What follows is a meditation on the meaning of friendship across borders, across mediums, across years. And the food that has nourished and continued to nourish it. Every band has a "friend-band"; every musician knows other musicians from their scene. This is an account of something deeper. *–LP*

Our first tour with the Japanese band Ghost was in 1995. They got off the plane from Japan in Chicago, having never been to the US, and they were hungry. We met them at O'Hare and went straight to a soul-food cafeteria. They were bewildered and overwhelmed. Some weeks later, sitting on the porch of a Cracker Barrel somewhere off a highway exit, Ghost bandleader Masaki Batoh looked wistful. "I miss soba," he said.

Restaurants are a part of touring life—musicians trade recommendations, swap horror stories, and develop sometimes-peculiar habits based on a career of hits and misses with meals on the road. But soul-food cafeterias and roadside pancake houses aren't the only way to eat in the US. Nor are conveyor-belt sushi places and ramen shops the only way to eat in Japan, for that matter. Many of our most memorable meals connected to music

Opposite: Post-show dinner in Misawa, Japan. Photo by Naomi Yang.

have taken place not in restaurants but in homes. And many have been shared with our friends from Japan.

The two of us grew up in families with powerful relationships to Japan. Damon's father, born in Poland to a Jewish family, escaped the Holocaust thanks to the courage of a Japanese diplomat in Lithuania, Chiune Sugihara, who bravely issued transit visas to Jews. Damon's grandparents, along with his then-nine-year-old father and infant aunt, lived in Japan for six months before finding further passage to the US.

Meanwhile, Naomi's father was born in Suzhou, outside Shanghai, and fled China during the Japanese invasion in the Second Sino-Japanese War—the family found safety in passage via Hong Kong to the UK, then eventually to the US. Both our families, taking opposite paths around the globe, settled within a mile or so of each other in New York. To one, the Japanese were saviors; to the other, they were the enemy. Japan was a charged place for both of us all our lives, and music is what finally allowed us to visit and discover it for ourselves.

When we first toured Japan—in 1995, shortly after Ghost's first US tour—we were hosted by a rock promotion company that took pride in choosing the kinds of restaurants they knew a foreign band would enjoy, many of which we did. But when that tour was over, we stayed extra time with our new friends in Ghost at their homes. And there we shared the beautiful, elemental foods they made for themselves on any given day. The same dynamic developed when members of Ghost came back to the US—they stayed with us for extended periods, and we cooked for them as we do for ourselves.

Something else developed between us and Ghost around food— an intimacy, more than just camaraderie. And since we come from different sides of the planet, that intimacy has shrunk the distance between us even when we are apart. We now think of our friends in Japan often at home in our own kitchen, as we reach for a jar of dried yuzu peel they sent or make dashi the way they taught us. Perhaps the same is true for them.

In this way, our food life with the extended Ghost family came to resemble the music we make together. We record at home in our living room, and so the albums we work on together have largely been catered by us, in our kitchen. Even on the road, we started gravitating toward a version of home cooking: exploring shops and markets for groceries, rather than looking for restaurants. One of the most memorable foods we ever tasted in Japan was a fig off a tree that had wandered just enough past its garden wall for Batoh to reach up and pick for us.

A surprise of Tokyo life, once we left the care of rock promoters and entered the homes of our musician friends, was how quiet and intimate its neighborhoods are. Ghost House was where Batoh lived when we first visited, on a quiet, narrow street off a sleepy cluster of shops by a train station. Once you get to know one of these village-like crossroads, the sprawling train map of Tokyo takes on a very different aspect— less New York City subway linking multiple urgencies and more rumbling, rambling lines through whistle-stop towns stretching hours away from the Shibuya or Shinjuku intersections pictured in every establishment shot of a band in Japan.

Sakura onigiri. Photo by Naomi Yang.

On that first visit, we stayed in Ghost House while our hosts necessarily continued their work life. In the middle of the day, there were hardly any sounds of people in the neighborhood, aside from passing bicycles or schoolchildren. Birds, cats (who wander in and out of houses in Japan, both their own and others), insects, the smells of burning mosquito coils and dashi cooking in other homes—this was a small-town Japanese environment we had no idea was out there but is in fact everywhere in Tokyo beyond the drunken boulevards near rock venues.

In their leisure time, our hosts took us to some favorite nearby places: a mountain with a monkey park, where we ate (what else?) soba. An old-fashioned sweets shop that served kakigori (shaved ice with beans on top). A temple with a family graveyard, where we gave water to the dead (because they are thirsty). But what stood out to us was how every night, no matter how late we came in or stayed up talking and listening to rare records, our friend Yumi prepared the next day's lunchtime bento boxes for everybody before bed. Rice and small savory dishes, to be accompanied of course by miso soup and green tea. It was like being in an Ozu film about the psychedelic underground.

As we returned to Japan on subsequent tours, the circle of homes that welcomed us widened. The larger group around Ghost began to spread out, some of them leaving Tokyo for their home-towns, building families or caring for elders. Bandmates shifted— Ghost eventually even ended—but the community that welcomed us continued to enlarge, and our ties with many deepened.

Iwao Yamazaki was the drummer on Ghost's first tour of the US, and while we didn't share much common language, we bonded with this earnest, elegant man with a mysteriously varied history: He had been a modern dancer and a rally-car driver, and he'd also worked in design and film. He plays drums and engineers recordings for experimental artists as well as psychedelic ones, and although he had already left Ghost before their next US tour, he remains close to many in their circle, and we continue to see him on all our visits to Japan.

One year, we were on tour in Japan shortly after New Year's, and Yamazaki's family invited us along with a number of our mutual musician friends to their home in Kawasaki to make mochi (pounded sticky rice) in the traditional manner. This is an ancient trust game, of a sort, between couples: The mochi sits cradled in a shallow wooden container, while the husband wields a heavy mallet and the wife reaches in to rotate the mashed rice ball between blows. The Yamazakis are experts but urged us all to try as well. Afterward, we ate a mochi feast prepared by Mrs. Yamazaki, a famous home cook: There was mochi with daikon radish, mochi with sweet black bean, and of course mochi in ozoni (New Year's soup).

Damon in Kyoto with Michio Kurihara. Photo by Naomi Yang.

Despite all the different seasons we have toured Japan—including typhoon season!—we never really get to choose our dates. And so only once have we had the good fortune to see the famous cherry blossoms. In 2013, our visit coincided with sakura season perfectly, so we got to enjoy not one but two hanami picnics under the flowering trees: one with Masaki Batoh and his family, prepared by Batoh's wife, Ritsuka; and one with our longtime touring and recording partner Michio Kurihara and his friend Emiko. Seeing the way our friends each approached this meal—and watching all the many other parties in the parks we visited, some clearly office gatherings, some romantic, some groups of students—made clear how tradition collides with individuality to make a million different hanami all part of one delirious celebration of an ephemeral moment.

What a place, that collectively honors a falling blossom! No wonder they seem to enjoy our melancholy music.

New Year's mochi pounding.
Photo by Naomi Yang.

Hanami picnic with Masaki Batoh's family. Photo by Naomi Yang.

Of all our Japanese friends, it is undoubtedly electric guitarist Michio Kurihara with whom we have shared the most meals. Starting in 2000, we began to tour as a trio with Kurihara, a live unit that became a happy collaboration for us all. Eventually we traveled many places together this way, including Kurihara's first tour of Europe, all our first visits to Brazil and Korea, and many places in the UK and the US. And Kurihara turned out to be an extraordinarily adventurous eater, from chipped beef on toast in a Baltimore diner to stinky tofu from a street cart in Taipei. Watching him eat even "boring" Western foods like fish and chips with mushy peas in Manchester is a special pleasure, as he approaches them with the same curiosity and thoroughness that he brings to trying new effects pedals.

But we have also had the chance to cook many meals for Kurihara in our home, as we record together (he has now played on six of our studio albums) or prepare for tour. Many of the meals we have shared with Kurihara have been functional, as time constraints during recording often dictate. But sometimes the ephemeral moment needs a celebration, like hanami. In the last days of 1999 and the first of 2000, as the millennium clicked over, we took time out of recording the album *Damon & Naomi with Ghost* to make a traditional Thanksgiving meal, since our friends had never tasted many of these very American foods. Most were a hit, but Yumi's comically horrified face when she first tasted cranberry sauce was unforgettable: "Is this food?" she asked.

Most recently, in the winter of 2019, we interrupted a tour of Japan to rent an apartment in Kyoto and take a few extra days just to be together with Kurihara and Emiko. She is a healer and prepared special teas for us all. This turned out to be our last tour before the pandemic, but it fortunately included time with Kurihara in a Tokyo studio, where he recorded electric guitar for what would become our 2021 album, *A Sky Record*.

It begins with a song called "Oceans in Between":

And how is the weather there
That warm, warm summer rain
Have you seen the fireflies
Are they glowing just the same

And when I think of you
Like the light from a distant star
Been a while since I've heard from you
I wonder how you are

And every day I think of you
I send all my strength to you
However long it's taking you
However long I'll wait for you

Is it telepathy
Or is it in my dreams
Can we hear the crickets sing
Though there are oceans in between

The Westar Travel Plaza off I-85 outside of Spartanburg, South Carolina. Photo by Luke Pyenson.

REST STOP: THE US

Off the highway in Wisconsin. Photo by Luke Pyenson.

What the US lacks in highway-side rest-stop culture, it more than makes up for in a genre known as "roadfood," a term coined by the once-married duo of Jane and Michael Stern in the late '70s. The pair cowrote several celebrated guidebooks and a column in *Gourmet* magazine on the subject and are considered among the nation's foremost authorities on regional cooking and roadside restaurant culture.

Mark Ibold, bassist of the seminal '90s indie-rock band Pavement (and *Lucky Peach*'s "Southeastern Pennsylvania correspondent") told us that the Sterns' *Eat Your Way Across the U.S.A.* was instrumental in steering Pavement toward several memorable meals on tour. As luck would have it, we were able to connect Mark and Michael by phone for a wide-ranging discussion about their shared experiences. The following is condensed and edited for clarity. *–LP*

Michael Stern: One of the reasons that we wrote *Roadfood,* and have done what we've done, and focused on the kind of restaurants that we focus on, is that it's our belief that you can really taste where you are—in the broadest sense of the word—in one-of-a-kind restaurants. If you go to chain restaurants, or even sort of formulaic restaurants, you could be anywhere. And I would imagine for somebody who's touring heavily, that could drive you insane!

I mean, you have no idea where you are, whereas if you go into a catfish parlor in Mississippi or a chowder house along the coast of Oregon, I don't wanna say it anchors you, but you're not just in a void; you're clearly in a particular place. You may just wanna eat, and the literal taste of the food is all you're gonna get, or you could talk to people, or not even talk but just listen to the accents of the people around you—it's a real way to get a genuine feel of where you are, not just someplace on the road.

Mark Ibold: Totally agree, and I think when I started going on tour—that was the early '90s—I think at that time, actually, a lot of bands weren't thinking that way. I don't think that they were thinking, like, "Oh, let's go and check out the local vibes at the catfish stand," or, you know, "the chili parlor." A lot of them wanted to have chain food.

But for my band, Pavement, it was wonderful to be able to pull over to places that were mostly recommended by you and Jane, and to actually sit back and check out the vibes of a small town, or a place in between two places that we were playing.

MS: Obviously fast food is thriving, and I think that for a lot of people, their sense of security comes from—you know what you're gonna get. And I think for many people, that's what gives them some sense of comfort.

For me, and, I think, hearing from you, it's your—I don't want to say comfort, but your sense of enjoyment comes from knowing you are someplace other than where you usually are, or where you were last night. The taste of the food is one thing, but beyond that, just that sense of actually experiencing a little sliver of life someplace—that makes me really happy. 'Cause I want to explore, and you can't do that by going into a McDonald's wherever you go, really.

MI: No, and you touched on something that I have always thought was very cool about your writing, which is that, you know, a lot of people will judge a place on the quality of the food, or the types of preparations, or whether they're using exotic ingredients and stuff like that. And I learned from going to some of those places that you recommended that it's not always about the food, you know? A lot of times it's just about the vibe.

MS: Totally.

MI: The food can be a wonderful part of it, but, you know, I go into a place and make the wrong order, and I'm eating a bland chicken-fried steak or something . . . If there are interesting people in there and I feel like I'm having a travel experience—a good travel experience—that's just so much more important to me, really, than the food. I mean, great food also makes a place memorable. But I feel like the vibe is very important.

MS: I totally agree. I used to have debates with some of the people in the food world, and I remember one guy in particular who said, "I don't care where I am; I don't care what's around me; all that matters to me is what's on that plate!" And I said, "I'm completely the opposite!"

Yes, what's on the plate matters—the better it tastes, the happier I am—but the whole point is to be in this wonderful environment, to talk to people, to listen to people, to look around, to look at those bulletin boards that a lot of restaurants have where people post things for sale, and upcoming events . . .

Both: [in unison] I love that!

MI: Or to be told that in order to use the bathroom, you have to walk through the kitchen . . .

MS: Oh yes, that's the greatest!

MI: Stuff like that is what really makes a place for me, and, I mean, how many times have you gone to a place where there are a bunch of people working in the kitchen who have all gone to culinary school, and they've all worked in fancy restaurants and everything, and they're making this meal for you that's actually pretty great, tastes great, but the vibe in the place is just . . . you don't wanna be there.

Eat Your Way Across the U.S.A. came out right before one of our big American tours, so we were just psyched, and we tried to go to as many places as we could if time allowed. That was at the point where we were not touring in a tour bus—we were able to drive ourselves—so we made some big detours. I remember Lambert's—

MS: Ah, home of the "throwed roll"!

MI: That was something that we read about in *Eat Your Way Across the U.S.A.*, and we were somewhat near it, but I think we made like a two-hour detour to go to this place, and I'll never forget it. When we walked into that place, it was just full of people, it was a huge space, I don't know if you remember it . . . ?

MS: Oh yeah!

MI: I was trying to make eye contact with the people who worked there, and they were all busy doing things, but then there was a guy on the complete other end of the place who kind of looked at me, and I waved to him. And when my hand went up in the air, he just threw this roll and it went straight into my palm. And I caught it from, I would say, at least fifty feet across the room.

MS: [*laughing*] What a great introduction to a restaurant!

MI: I remember looking into my hands, like, dumbfounded, and I was trying to tell my bandmates that a guy had just thrown this roll—I mean, nobody even saw it, it happened so quickly—and I was about to tell my bandmates that this had just happened when another one came flying at us and hit our drummer right in the face!

MS: [*laughing*]

MI: And then everybody just started cracking up, and somebody came over and gave us a table. I think they served everything in giant cast-iron pans, just, like, ridiculous portions with meat slopping over them, just gigantic, and I think once you sat down, for your rolls, they brought you these little tubs of . . . what's it called? It's not maple syrup . . . it's not honey . . .

MS: Sorghum, or molasses . . .

MI: Sorghum, sorghum, yeah. I'll never forget that. It was just wonderful, and it was a great detour. I mean, we were just going between two big cities to play shows, and we got to do that!

The Hooksett Welcome Center off I-93 in New Hampshire. One of the best rest areas in the US. Photo by Luke Pyenson.

MS: You know, now there are several Lambert's, and it's become sort of a theme-parky place. You went to the original one [in Sikeston, Missouri], when it was really unique and great, but as I recall—maybe I'm wrong—but in my mind, you got your rolls, and then they would just come by with a *bucket*, and take a ladle, and just pour the sorghum onto your table, you know? Like on the table, you sort of wipe your roll . . . I might be wrong about that, but that's what I remember! [*laughing*]

MI: [*laughing*] That's great! I wonder if they'll be doing that post-Covid?

So how long would your trips be [with Jane]? Would it just be the two of you? And would you bring anybody else along?

MS: Our trips were probably shorter than what you guys mostly do. In the very beginning we would sometimes go out for three weeks or four, but after a while we would kind of burn out. It was always the two of us, but one occasion later on in our career we took somebody with us. It was a huge mistake, and the guy we took with us—we were in Albuquerque and he had a room and we had a room, and this was after maybe just a week on the road—we got up the next morning and went to the desk, and they said, "Oh, your friend checked out!"

MI: Oh my god! Albuquerque was actually one of my all-time favorite recommendations from you guys, and it was called, all I remember is "Sanitary Tortilla . . ."

MS: Oh, the M&J Sanitary Tortilla company!

MI: Oh my god. What a wonderful place that was.

MS: It was so great, and that's one of those—obviously this happens all the time—but when that went out of business, I *wept*. 'Cause that was always the first place we went to when we got to Albuquerque.

MI: One thing that I think is sort of a funny thing I've noticed is that a lot of great places are just two letters, like I guess the owners' names or whatever. Do you have anything to say about that? [*laughing*]

MS: I never even thought of that as a theme, but I immediately think of G&R Tavern in Waldo, Ohio, actually.

MI: In which part of Ohio?

MS: It's sort of in the Ohio River valley. But G&R Tavern makes the world's greatest bologna sandwich. I mean, they make their own bologna . . .

MI: Oh, god.

MS: I mean, it's nothing like the tasteless bologna you get in the supermarkets!

MI: There's a place that you recommended in El Paso—a Mexican restaurant that's in a gas station called H&H, I think?

MS: It's a car wash.

MI: Yes, a car wash, sorry, and that place was a mindblower. Delicious food and just really one of the most killer vibes. I think it's dependable, from my experience, places that have two letters with the ampersand between them, they're generally pretty solid . . . [*laughing*]

MS: I'm sure if we worked at it, we could think of a whole bunch of others!

MI: I think that this interest among people who are in bands—I think it's really affected bands more recently. What I remember from running into other musicians on the road was *no* interest in that stuff, and people that were very fussy about food. Now I think a lot of bands think of it as kind of a cool thing to be able to say, "Yeah, we went and we had ribs in Memphis, and they were fantastic; we actually took the time to stop and get them."

But that wasn't really a big deal to many people in the early Pavement days, and it just seems weird to me 'cause it doesn't seem like *that* long ago. But a lot has changed since then.

MS: Dramatically.

MI: If I would ask people in towns where to go to eat . . . I just had to give up, you know? And you can't ask a person at a hotel, 'cause they just tell you to go where the tourists wanna go. So, god, I mean, that book really made a huge difference for us!

MS: Well, thank you, I appreciate that, I really do, thanks! I've loved talking with you.

MI: Loved talking to you, too, and thank you so much for doing this. And just, keep up the good work. It's just helped me so much over the years, and really made me happy.

Talking Heads at La Coupole

by Chris Frantz (Talking Heads; Tom Tom Club)

What's more romantic than a young American band's first meal on tour in Paris? The bill from Frankie Cosmos's is framed in my kitchen—though Lauren and I don't need any help jogging our memory.

It was the first stop of our first-ever tour in Europe, and we arrived a night early. The evening feels surreal even now. At a bistro in the Latin Quarter, we shared radishes with salted butter and warm artichoke petals arranged around tender artichoke hearts cloaked in vinaigrette. My main course was, I still believe, the perfect jet-lag dinner: an omelette aux fines herbes and a bracing salad. We ordered every dessert on the menu and went to bed buzzing.

This is, however, the most sedate and boring story on earth compared with the following essay, by Talking Heads drummer, Tom Tom Club mastermind, and esteemed memoirist Chris Frantz. We're very grateful to him for sharing it. *—LP*

During the recording of our first album, *Talking Heads: 77*, we received a call from Ken Kushnick at Sire Records asking if we'd like to support the Ramones on a tour of Europe and the UK. We didn't have to think about it very long. We said yes, you bet we would!

Our first show ever was opening for the Ramones at CBGB, and it was a doozy of a double bill. Musically and aesthetically, our two bands were complete opposites, but the show *really* worked. It was the best of both worlds. Not every Ramones fan liked Talking Heads, but most of them did. We found that the European audiences were so thirsty for the sounds of the new bands from Lower Manhattan that the kids lined up to hear us play.

In those days, the beautiful spring of 1977, our record companies would actually give us tour support, which, of course, they hoped to recoup from our record royalties. This enabled us to tour properly and stay in mostly cheap hotels. We also played some fabulous venues.

Le Bataclan, on the Boulevard Voltaire, is a greatly loved historic theater. It opened in 1865. So many great artists had performed there, from Colette to Buffalo Bill Cody, Maurice Chevalier to the Velvet Underground. Our show was a smashing success. Some crazy punks set off smoke bombs in the lobby, but otherwise it was cool. Talking Heads delivered our message and set the stage for the Ramones, who were already worshipped and adored by the French underground rock crowd.

Toward the end of the Ramones' set, two drag queens climbed up on either side of the stage and suggestively danced le jerk and le boogaloo to "Blitzkrieg Bop." It was so much fun, and both bands made their mark in Parisian rock history that night. After the show, our man at Phonogram, a guy named Jackie, invited both bands and crew out to dinner. We accepted with pleasure.

After packing up our gear with our British crew, we all piled into the bus. It wasn't a tour bus; it was a *tourist* bus with about twenty double seats. Our driver, Paul, who was a nineteen-year-old bus mechanic from London on his first trip to continental Europe, drove across the Seine and up the Boulevard Raspail to the corner of the Boulevard du Montparnasse, where Rodin's statue of Balzac is, and turned right. Halfway down the block on the opposite side of the street was our destination, the famous brasserie and bar américain La Coupole.

Opened in 1927, La Coupole was an instant hit with the arts and literary crowd. You could walk into the huge, glamorous art deco interior and dine alongside some of the most important artists of all time. We're talking about Jean Cocteau, Alberto Giacometti, Josephine Baker, Man Ray, Georges Braque, Brassaï, Pablo Picasso, Simone de Beauvoir and Jean-Paul Sartre, André Malraux, Jacques Prévert, Marc Chagall, Edith Piaf, Ernest Hemingway, Marlene Dietrich, Ava Gardner, Serge Gainsbourg, and Jane Birkin! Albert Camus celebrated his Nobel Prize in literature here with his friends. After this night, Talking Heads and the Ramones could be added to the list.

The restaurant is vast, with high ceilings and rectangular columns painted by students of Henri Matisse and some lesser-known artists of the period. There is always an enormous arrangement of flowers in the center of the room. The lighting is bright but not uncomfortably so. There is plenty of space and air. There are mosaics in the ceiling. It's not overly fancy. It's perfect.

Our party of sixteen was led to a long table in a far corner. The Ramones sat at one end, and Talking Heads sat at the other with Jackie, our tour manager Mickey Stewart, and the crew in the middle. Champagne and beer were served immediately. Everybody was in high spirits after a fantastic show. Even Johnny Ramone, a chronic complainer, was beaming. He was looking forward to steak frites. In fact, most of us ordered the steak frites, but while Johnny had his well done, our Scottish soundman, Frank Gallagher, when asked how he'd like his cooked, exclaimed, "Arrrgh, just wipe its ass!"

As an appetizer, we in Talking Heads ordered the escargots in the shell with a hot butter and garlic sauce. I'd never eaten escargots before, but I was feeling adventurous, and they were delicious. Tina was happy we both had the escargots: The garlic butter was intense. I had my steak rare and au poivre. It was tender and juicy; the frites were perfectly golden and crisp.

For dessert, Jackie ordered fresh strawberries and whipped cream for the table. So perfect. Everyone was feeling convivial and content when all of a sudden the two drag queens who had been go-go dancing onstage with the Ramones appeared. One of them took special notice of Paul, the young driver, and sat down on his lap.

Paul had just been telling Tina that he'd like to bring his new bride to Paris on a holiday. Now Paul was blushing bright pink and trying to squirm away, but his new admirer was not having it. She was in control. She said, "Paul, do you like fraises? *Moi, j'adore les fraises!*" Our eyes widened as she raised her blouse and painted herself suggestively with whipped cream. She asked again, "Paul, do you like fraises?" With that she pressed herself toward Paul's face. Our tour manager Mickey, clearly seeing Paul's embarrassment, told everyone the party was over, *now*!

Tina and I have returned to La Coupole over the years with our family and friends, even with our two beagles. Well-behaved dogs are always welcome. Years later, when we were in Paris recording the *Naked* album, we had an apartment just around the corner on the Boulevard Raspail. We'd eat at La Coupole frequently and always happily—but the memory of our first dinner there lingers vividly, and what a great dinner it was! Not only was the food and wine sumptuous, but the company was so much fun. We didn't get to eat often with the Ramones—they mostly preferred fast food when they were on the road. But on this one unforgettable night in Paris, we all dined together at La Coupole.

Flora and Fauna

by Meg Duffy (Hand Habits)

Before I ever played in a band that anyone cared about, it was always my dream to perform at Iceland Airwaves. Even just the name conjured a sublime image of indie music undulating like the northern lights above a fairy-tale landscape. My Iceland Fever only intensified when I first visited the country in 2010, as a college sophomore.

After leaving my first remotely successful band to attend grad school, I resigned myself to the reality that I'd probably never play Airwaves. Instead, I wrote a paper about the festival following a weeklong study trip to Iceland. But unbelievably, my Airwaves journey didn't end with this paper. Two years later, I was playing at the 2016 edition with Frankie Cosmos and—corny but true—fulfilling my fantasy. The only things better than our two shows were the meals full of fresh fish, pristine Icelandic dairy, and great quantities of dill.

As it happens, the brilliant musician Meg Duffy, who performs as Hand Habits, was also at Airwaves in 2016, having a somewhat different culinary experience. I'm a Food Person who came of age in the Time of Noma, so I'm used to fawning accounts of eating in the Nordic region (and have even been responsible for some). It's refreshing, as this piece shows, to hear another point of view. *–LP*

In the fall of 2016, I was playing in Kevin Morby's band, and we were booked to begin a monthlong European tour with a performance at Iceland Airwaves. Iceland had always seemed inaccessible to me—too distant even for my imagination—but Kevin suggested spending a few days in Reykjavík before the festival to experience the beauty of this enigmatic country. My first glimpses of the Icelandic countryside came through the windows of the airport shuttle: a murky, gray-green sky reflecting back off the snow-covered ground. I was jet-lagged and half-asleep, but it already felt surreal to be here to play a festival. I was twenty-six and had barely traveled outside New York State before meeting Kevin and joining his band. We had toured in Europe and the UK the year before, but this felt like another world entirely.

And yet—immediately upon landing I ran into my friend Oliver from the band Pavo Pavo, carting around massive flight cases in a similar state of jet-lagged haze. Years later, Oliver would join Kevin's band, and we'd reminisce about the strangeness of this encounter so far from home. Touring does this to you—ejects you from your comfort zone and catapults you into what always feels so alien and distant. But you always end up running into the same bands whose touring schedules seem to crisscross your own. The bonds that form this way can be both quick and lifelong.

We spent our days off exploring Reykjavík and the nature that surrounds it. Our little crew—the band plus Kevin's manager, his agent, and a tagalong friend that none of us had met before—went to a geothermal spa at the edge of a mostly frozen lake to calm our fraught nerves (this was weeks before the 2016 election). We oscillated between sweating out our jet lag in the dry heat of picturesque saunas and cooling ourselves in the icy waters of the lake.

When everyone decided to indulge in the spa's buffet of smoked fish and other local delights, I opted to wait for the familiar comfort of a grayish hot dog at a gas station on the way back into the city. Shortly before the tour, I'd spent most of my savings moving across the country, and my attitude toward eating on tour was: What's the cheapest thing I can buy that will make me feel full?

On North American tours, it would be hot dogs from Love's with mayonnaise, relish, mustard, and a tiny bit of ketchup. I also loved post-show dollar street tacos when I could find them. Many nights, I scavenged the green room for rider leftovers, bringing coolers

The Icelandic countryside. Photo by Meg Duffy.

packed with Sabra hummus and cold cuts into the van. This way, I wouldn't have to waste the previous night's ten-dollar dinner buyouts on the Whole Foods hot bar. Back then, the idea of flying on a plane over the ocean to play music was already the height of extravagance, never mind spending over fifteen dollars for lunch.

After a few days, we left behind our bliss and plunged deeper into the guts of the city and the festival that takes it over each November. A perennial stop for up-and-coming indie musicians, Iceland Airwaves is sort of like a European SXSW, with bands performing throughout Reykjavík in venues large and small, to audiences made up of both fans and industry types. But keep in mind: Reykjavík's population is about an eighth of Austin's. During Airwaves, the tiny seaside city is buzzing with activity.

Our show took place in a massive indoor sports arena that hosts some of Reykjavík's professional soccer, basketball, and handball teams. After the deep silence and beauty of snow-covered rural Iceland, it was jarring to be in this type of setting again. I definitely didn't have my touring muscles up to strength yet. PJ Harvey was headlining our venue, and her dressing room was right next to ours. After our set, which I seem to have no memory

Downtown Reykjavik. Photo by Luke Pyenson.

of, I could hear her band rehearsing before marching through the crowd like a drum line, carrying big bass drums.

We worked up quite a hunger throughout the long day of soundchecking, performing, loading in and out, and finally taking in the fanfare of PJ Harvey. We all did our best to keep our hunger at bay, comforted by the expectation of a nice communal meal in the city after the show. But since it was the weekend—and during the festival—almost all of Reykjavík's restaurants were booked solid. The only place that could seat all eight of us was an experimental New Nordic restaurant in the basement of a brewery. It was very expensive and offered only one tasting menu. I had never had a tasting menu before.

I remember the disclaimer we all received from our manager when they confirmed the reservation: If any of us were not comfortable spending this kind of money—around 120 dollars each—we could absolutely opt out and find something more reasonable. No pressure to stay! But since we were all starving and in that gray-area touring mindset somewhere between work and vacation, we all agreed we were up for it despite the dollar signs. Why not treat ourselves to a nice fancy meal?

When we sat down, the waiters began explaining the menu, which featured ingredients that—at least to me—sounded like they'd be more at home in a biology textbook. Flora and fauna. Someone in our crew said, "If anyone wants to bail, please feel free!" But everyone agreed to stay despite mounting hesitations. My belly was growling, and I figured I'd feel full with seven courses ahead of us. In fact, I even feared being *too* full by the fifth course!

The first course arrived, and I swear I thought someone was playing a practical joke on us. It was a quarter-sized piece of burnt chicken skin with a tendril of dried moss or lichen on it. Second course: one single wild carrot and two flakes of sea salt. Third course (twenty minutes later), everyone's hunger now manifesting as manic smiles and raised eyebrows: a tiny fermented quail egg on a bed of hay. Fourth course, and we're all losing it in the damp basement, silent and sectioned off with a red curtain, blond-haired servers dancing in and out of sight: a tiny mushroom cap with compost-tasting muck stuffed inside. Sixth course: one single drop of cream the size of a dime on a slate slab.

At some point in the dinner, the unknown friend of a friend—still a part of our crew yet still random—started to huff and puff (probably hunger-induced agitation), going after the person in our crew who had suggested the restaurant. This despite the multiple disclaimers and opt-outs, and despite everyone's mutual agreement! As if an already awkward meal couldn't get any more

A hot dog stand in Reykjavík. Photo by Luke Pyenson.

uncomfortable, there were now accusations being thrown around from one end of the table to the other. Amid this tension, dessert came: a single shaving of dark chocolate sprinkled with cinnamon.

Our manager gracefully and I'd imagine a bit spitefully decided to pick up the entire bill—somewhere in the neighborhood of a thousand dollars—which embarrassed the unwelcome guest and left us all with mouths agape. I left feeling loopy and hungrier, somehow, than when I'd entered. We laughed about this "fine dining" experience as we spilled back out onto the streets of Reykjavík.

Before long, the Icelandic equivalent of a 7-Eleven beckoned, and I found myself gravitating toward the steamy, spinning hot dogs behind the counter. It cost me four krónur, and I loaded it up with all the complimentary fixings. As I sat happily on the curb, I laughed thinking that there were probably as many bites in the hot dog as there had been courses in that hypercurated, high-class meal.

I enjoyed every one of them.

PROMOTER SPOTLIGHT: ANDRÉ GOMES

André at dinner. Photo courtesy of André Gomes.

André Gomes is a concert promoter and a music writer who has put on shows in Porto under the banner of the Portuguese webzine *Bodyspace,* and in Auditório de Espinho, next to Porto, where he works. He is exactly who you want to meet on the road. Real Estate had been in Lisbon for a gig, and I decided to spend some time on my own exploring northern Portugal. When our mutual friend Kevin Morby found out that I was in Porto, he texted me, "You have to meet André!" Fifteen minutes later he was on the other end of my telephone, and an hour after that he was regaling me with stories at a popular local bar.

I had come to Porto armed with a list of things to do in the city lifted directly from a cheesy *New York Times* article. When I ordered a Porto Tonico at the bar, doing my best to blend in with the locals, André laughed at me. We stayed at the bar for a few hours and then wound up in somebody's dining room, enjoying good wine and a home-cooked meal. I didn't know until days later that André did not know these people any better than I did. I threw out my list—I didn't need it anymore; I had André. I spent every day with him and was blessed by his hospitality, his generosity, and his cooking! We talked endlessly about music, about food, and about the future of his beautiful country. I understand now that these things, to him, are inextricably linked. *-AB*

Portugal à Mesa (Portugal at the Table)

by André Gomes, *Bodyspace*
Porto, Portugal

Translated from the original Portuguese by Luke Pyenson

It's easy, almost inevitable, to romanticize the lives of touring artists. Sometimes it's nearly impossible to see past the glamor of the stage, the excitement of getting to know a new city each day or thousands of new people each week. But those of us who've been involved in curating, producing, or promoting concerts know perfectly well that this lifestyle isn't always as glamorous as it may seem. Going on tour for weeks on end can be an exhausting experience—both at the physical and emotional levels. And sometimes—between tight schedules, problems with back-line, depression, homesickness, missing loved ones—a meal can be a veritable life raft.

Over the past several years, I've hosted and cooked for dozens of artists at my house; I've taken another hundred or so out for lunch or dinner.

I've seen with my own eyes, and felt in my bones, the type of sincerity and emotion that you feel only when people come together around a table replete with good food, especially when what unites them is music. I've shared meals with musicians at the beginning of their tours and at the end, immediately before and right after important elections, on holidays and humdrum weekdays, as preludes to full and empty performances. In short: on good days and bad (and everything in between).

Our encounters are often fleeting in the literal sense (they can last half a day or less), but it's not unheard of for them to spawn yearslong friendships. It's not as if food is uniquely responsible for this, but certainly it's around the table that we have our most memorable and lucid conversations. Something about gathering for a meal brings out our truest selves and helps us lower our guards. And something about the intimacy of sharing food, which usually happens among friends and family, seems to expedite friendships among those who've just met. I remember a good friend, a singer and violinist, who was brought to tears by the infallible combination of gustatory and aural pleasure caused by, respectively, a wonderful meal and one of those life-changing records. I'll never forget it.

Often, at these lunches and dinners, conversation turns to Portuguese fado. Not the music, that is, but the inevitability—*fado* literally means "fate"—of this country. I'll talk about our fragile pride as a nation, and all the incredible things that are very much ours, and that the world knows as Portuguese but that we've historically been too scared to sell. From incredible yet inexpensive wine to olive oil, from conservas to the beloved cod we crave (that doesn't actually exist in our own vast waters), to traditional sweets and pastries whose roots can be traced back to the humble monasteries and convents making magic out of sugar, egg yolks, almonds, and not much else. I talk about our gastronomy—its incredible diversity, and the pride that we take, without reservation, in preparing, savoring, talking about, showing off, and sometimes even bragging about it.

For all of these reasons, it doesn't seem too risky for me to declare: Food is a strong part of Portuguese identity (whatever that means). And naturally, the Portuguese art of hospitality—so often on full display around the table and so often praised by artists and others—is nothing less than a national treasure that needs to be preserved. I've often shared my fear that, as has happened in other countries, mass tourism could put this legacy at risk. But even stronger is my resolve to play a part— through showing visiting musicians the very best we have to offer—in safeguarding it.

Portugal is quite a small country that, at times, seems to be stuck in the past. But it punches above its weight when it serves, for example, a perfectly grilled piece of fish. When it brings a texturally perfect caldo verde to the table. When it arranges six perfectly golden-brown bolinhos de bacalhau just so on a serving platter. When it sprinkles fresh cilantro over an açorda that has been labored over and refined up to the last moment. And that's no small thing!

I traveled a lot before the pandemic hit, and I always insisted on bringing my palate with me. I've been moved many times—squid-ink risotto in Croatia, green curry in Thailand, bobó de camarão in Brazil, the simplest pastas in Florence, baked feta in Greece—but I am equally moved at home in Portugal when I eat sea bass baked in a salt crust, arroz de mariscos, grilled limpets, polvo à lagareiro, and other dishes I grew up with (literally and metaphorically) over the years.

I've always known, but only recently put together, that my paternal grandfather was a violinist and my maternal grandfather was a farmer. Although they were very different, I'd like to believe they would have found common ground around the table, sharing good food and music with each other. I wouldn't say I believe in destiny, but part of me wants to believe this is all connected.

André at lunch. Photo by Alex Bleeker.

Pide, Mannheim

by Ethan Bassford (Ava Luna)

Ethan Bassford, the bassist of consummate New York City art-pop band Ava Luna, has a particular way of walking when he's on his way to eat something he's excited about. It's as if he's constantly peering around a corner, overtaken by the anticipation of a good meal. I trust his taste in food instinctively, and he's one of my favorite people to eat with.

In this essay, we meet Ethan in Mannheim, Germany, after an early festival set, walking around town trying to find a place to eat. I can't tell you how many times I've been in Ethan's shoes, specifically because Frankie Cosmos never headlined festivals—we always played in the late afternoon or early evening. We frequently had time off in random European cities with nothing to do but walk around, taking in the vibe and looking for a good meal.

When I think back to my fondest memories of tour, they're often pretty similar to this one. I bet Ethan remembers his Mannheim festival set, and I remember all our festival sets too—but the languid spring and summer afternoons exploring towns I'd never heard of (Primošten, Croatia, and Hyères, France, come to mind) will always be among the best of my life. *-LP*

In Mannheim, we're done with the gig early. It was a daytime festival at a nearby racetrack, Maifeld Derby, and since we're not that big a deal, our set was in the afternoon. We're four shows into our European tour, and we're starting to feel that special sort of tightness you get from playing in front of people every night after being in one another's company all day. Feeling accomplished, and having stayed up entirely too late the night before, we are excited to settle into our lodging a little early.

Seeing a café just across the street, I lead a small party to grab an espresso. The woman who gets up to serve us doesn't seem to understand any English, but I know enough German to say what I think is "One espresso, please." *Ein Espresso, bitte.* Later I will check and learn that *einen* is the correct declension in this scenario, for grammatical reasons that escape me. I always feel like an asshole not being able to communicate when I travel, but of the languages on this tour, I'm most comfortable with German, thanks to a class I took on nineteenth-century lieder. But Franz Schubert and Robert Schumann are not so helpful for everyday conversation. I remember how to say "When you say 'I love you,'

I weep bitterly" and "Deep in my heart I shudder," but not "Where's the bathroom?"

The espresso arrives, and it is perfect. Strong, earthy, neither bitter nor acidic—it is rare to get this good of a pull even at the fanciest coffee shops back home. If I hadn't already gorged myself on the beers and Club-Mate on offer at Maifeld Derby, I would want to come back later to have a drink. But I'm done with beers for the day and a little sleepy. I was up late last night for no real reason, just watching bad TV in the hotel room, unable to get tired enough. We're done here for now. Espressos finished, we walk outside to find our bandmate Becca deep into a dance contest with a gaggle of smiling children.

Eventually the party breaks up (everybody won) and we find our way to the rental apartment where we'll spend the night. I briefly consider turning in, but I want to take a walk first, and several of us want to eat something. We were fed well at the gig: chicken schnitzel, red cabbage, gnocchi, lasagna. Competently executed steam-table food, and plenty of it. But this was a daytime gig; dinner was earlier than usual, and we'll probably be up for a bit. Turkish is the obvious move. Most of the good late-night food in Germany is Turkish, and this time we're even in a Turkish neighborhood.

Consulting my phone, I find a place half a mile away that looks good: Uzun Taşfırını. It appears to be a bakery, and not being quite hungry enough for a full meal, I'm thinking something like a spinach pie is just the ticket. They look delicious in the photos. My bandmates Carlos and Becca come along for the ride. If we hustle, we can get to this place twenty minutes before it closes and take whatever they have left to go. Cutting it close, but doable.

The air is a perfectly cool-enough temperature, and even though it's half past nine, it's still light out. It's beautiful and disorienting. Our path takes us through a plaza with benches and a playground, and it's buzzing with activity. Some kids are running around, and adults of all ages are sitting and talking, some with drinks. I get a strong sense-memory, a very specific feeling I haven't felt since I was a kid in the Bronx.

Our building had three steps that led down to the entrance to form an inward-facing stoop, and we would spend summer nights there with a rotating cast of neighbors. We'd run up and down the block, bouncing a ball around or drawing on the sidewalks with chalk while our parents sat on steps or curbs or lawn chairs, shooting the shit and watching the sun go down. It was a convivial, unstructured neighborhood hang for whoever was around, and that looks like the situation here. The light is the same, ditto how the air smells. The way sound travels. I feel why all those kids wanted to dance.

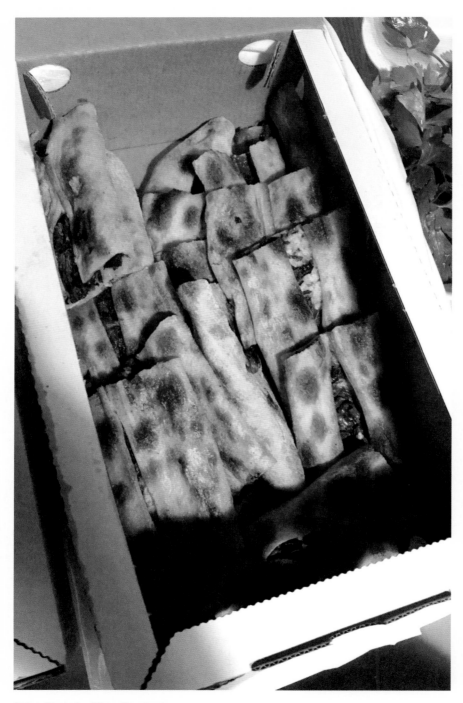

Pides. Photo by Ethan Bassford.

On the block by the bakery a crowd has gathered, eight or ten people standing around a car. Getting closer, we see what the fuss is about: A crow is on the hood. The owner of the car is holding a piece of bread to try to entice it to move, and a passerby is opening the hood to see if the movement will make the crow fly away. Others are trying various cajoling and threatening gestures, to no avail. It's the damnedest thing; the crow just wants to be on the hood of the car and will not be dissuaded. Or is it stuck? It doesn't look stuck, but someone reaches over to move the windshield wiper and see if that does something. No dice. People are helping and the bakery is about to close, so we keep moving.

Entering the bakery, my heart sinks. The lights are on, but the display is empty, save one longish piece of lahmaçun, a flatbread thinly spread with spiced ground meat. I love lahmaçun, but it's not what we came for, and there's definitely not enough for the three of us. In the back I see some nice-looking bread but no pies, and also no one behind the counter. Are we too late? Shit.

Becca rings the bell on the counter and two guys emerge from the back. I ask what they still have, hoping there's some stock of pies just outside our view. They can't understand my question at all, and I have no idea how to convey it in German. One guy asks a question, which I assume is "What do you want?" With some reading, pointing, and finger counting, we manage to convey that we want five spinach pies, thinking of the little hand-sized things you might get back home. Two things start to become clear: They're going to make our spinach pies from scratch, and the pies are easily the length and width of an adult human arm.

Watching the pies come together is captivating. The dough is delicate and stretchy, and the baker forms an oblong shape before laying a thick, even sheet of spinach atop it. The spinach looks freshly chopped, a far cry from the thawed mulch you so often get in similar baked goods. He sprinkles a couple of handfuls of a crumbly white cheese across each and then pinches the sides in to form little spinach canoes, sealed only at the ends and at a few points across their length to leave much of the filling exposed. A giant wood oven blazes behind him. One of the other guys notices my interest and motions for me to come behind the counter by the oven to see up close, and I'm moved by the generosity of this small gesture.

I can't see the oven's whole interior, but it looks as big as a twin bed. The bottom is lined with rectangular slabs of stone. The burning wood sits on one side rather than in the back, and the pies are placed a couple of feet away from it two at a time. Halfway through, the baker uses a tool like a long, thin pizza peel to remove the pies and rotate them so they heat evenly. His movements are practiced and precise, and it's a pleasure to watch. Not wanting to be in the way, I thank him and go back to the table to wait. I learn that in Turkish the pies are called pides.

The guy behind the counter asks if we want to take some more food, and it looks like they're referring to the slab of lahmaçun we saw coming in. Why yes, we do, *danke*! Do we want some fresh bread too? Sure, why not! We are all eating entirely too much bread in Europe, but this stuff will all get thrown out (or fed to the crows) if we don't take it. Maybe we'll even save ourselves a food stop tomorrow. The baker removes our pides from the oven, brushes them with something we can't see, and chops them into palm-sized slices with a cleaver. Finally, he loads them into brick-shaped rectangular boxes labeled "pizza."

There ends up being only four pides, not five, which is a relief. They look sort of like open-faced calzones, but up close they are mostly filling, the dough paper-thin. There are also four Styrofoam containers of assorted fixings. In addition to the pides we are given the lahmaçun I saw when we walked in—also paper-thin and chopped into rectangles—and several long loaves of a beautiful flatbread with a raised crust around the edge like pizza. It is the same oblong shape as the pides, but thicker and fluffier. Carlos gets a water, and I take a chance on ayran, a salty yogurt drink I've always seen at these places but never tried. The whole heap is around thirty euros.

This is as fruitful a food journey as I could have hoped for, and a way more hospitable reception than we deserved, considering the circumstances. The guys look amused by our guileless fascination with everything that is happening. They probably think we're high. I wish I had the words to express my gratitude: how this is exactly the sort of experience I am seeking when I venture out for food in a new place, how they didn't merely feed me but really made my day, how they gave me a sweet memory of being welcomed. I can just smile broadly and say, "*Danke, danke schön, gute Nacht.*"

The plan was to eat in the courtyard of our rental apartment's building, but we decide to go back to the plaza. It's clearly public, and there are lights and benches and tables. There are so many people, some who might even like a snack. As we walk, I attempt to use Google Translate to determine how you offer food to a plaza full of strangers in German.

The pides are transcendent. The dough is impressively thin, with a pleasant springy texture, dotted with black blisters from the heat. The spinach is cooked just enough, as precisely as though it were blanched, and the salty, fatty cheese offsets it beautifully. The fixings turn out to be fresh parsley, pickled hot peppers, and slices of lemon. I wish there were more peppers, but even just the parsley and lemon do something special on this pie, adding brightness and a surprising depth of flavor. Despite their intimidating size, we eat just short of three easily. The lahmaçun is also excellent, with the same thin dough and a heavily spiced ground-meat topping. The ayran is delicious too, perfectly complementing the food with lactic tang.

Shortly before we finish, a small group of youngish middle-aged men fills up the table behind us. They brought beer, but the vibe is mellow. Becca goes over to offer them some of our food, and because we're unable to explain our circumstances, I can't imagine what they think. Regardless, the men look very happy with the unexpected gift. They are all smiles, and they thank us profusely.

Bitte schön, you're welcome; I know that one too.

Breakfast with GL

a recollection with The Beths

Fans of New Zealand's The Beths may already know that bassist Ben Sinclair fastidiously documents every breakfast the band eats on tour on his blog (www.breakfastandtravelupdates.com). It was thus no surprise that the group chose to relay a breakfast story for this collection, and their chosen format—a self-annotated-and-transcribed conversation—works perfectly to convey their collective charm and dry Kiwi humor.

We meet The Beths on tour in Cleveland—bands are constantly in Ohio—where their friend Rachel Lawrence steps in as sound engineer for the night. Bands unable to tour with a full-time sound engineer usually rely upon "house" engineers at each venue, the skill and disposition of whom can be wildly variable. When a friend does sound, everything seems right with the universe, and we can focus on playing and enjoying the show.

The Beths trace the feeling of hospitality from the venue to Rachel's parents' house, where they're guests for the evening. Rachel's dad happens to be the owner/operator of a local diner, so it's a post-show breakfast that lives on in Beths lore. And just a quick note: When they say *t-sauce*, they mean "tomato sauce." Which, in their part of the world, means ketchup. *–LP*

We begin by setting the scene.

Liz Stokes: Set the scene, Ben.

Ben Sinclair: We'd just played at the Beachland Ballroom in Cleveland, not the small room, in the big room. It was the middle of winter and we'd been on tour for weeks, months even. This was the icy tour.

Jon Pearce: It was. I remember after the ballroom show we played some cricket in the car park in the snow.

BS: Oh yeah, that's right.

JP: A bit of snow cricket.

In this next sentence, Microsoft Word suggests replacing our humble comma with a semicolon.

BS: We played some snow cricket; it was very cold. We had invited Rachel Lawrence to the gig. She did our monitors on a previous tour, and this was her hometown. Somehow she ended up doing our front-of-house sound.

JP: I didn't know she did that until after the gig.

LS: Really?!?

JP: Yeah, 'cause we soundchecked with someone else, the house person.

BS: She literally turned up and decided to mix it.

LS: Well, people can't just decide to do that—it's because that's her local venue and she was really tight with the people.

BS: Anyway, when you have only one American friend and you turn up in their town and they come and mix your gig, it's a nice feeling.

LS: Yeah, she was great.

JP: It was a real following-through of American hospitality offers.

BS: That was how great her hospitality was. When we were on tour with Death Cab in Europe, she said, "You know, anytime you're passing through Cleveland, y'all can stay at my place," and then we did.

LS: Yeah, we literally did.

At this point, Tristan, who was waiting patiently on the sidelines, steps in with a warm and succinct summary of our feelings so far.

Tristan Deck: It was such a hugely inspirational act of paying it forward, I reckon. It made me think of my home and all the things I'd like to share with someone traveling through who was far from home on a long tour.

BS: It was pretty late by the time we got out, and I'm trying to remember how talked-up this meal was. I feel like Rachel talked it up on the Death Cab tour, like, "You should come over and my dad will cook you a meal!"

JP: That's what I remember as well, and it really escalated on the drive home. It wasn't, I think, until we finally met GL (Rachel's dad) that I realized that he actually owns and operates a local diner of some repute.

BS: I know he runs a coffee shop, or maybe he used to run a diner, or maybe he serves food at his coffee shop. He's a man that knows his way around a griddle.

JP: Oh, god, yeah. A hospitable man.

GL runs the Lakeshore Coffee House. Open since 1992.

LS: What was on the menu?

BS: So we got there, and we were offered pancakes, chocolate pancakes.

TD: Chocolate pancakes.

BS: I think french toast.

JP: And omelets. In my mind it was a choice, you know, to have pancakes, or chocolate pancakes, or omelets, or, um, the other thing . . . [*clicking fingers as he thinks*]

LS: Waffles—no, there weren't waffles—french toast?

TD: French toast.

JP: French toast. In fact the choice was nothing or omelets, french toast, pancakes, and chocolate pancakes.

LS: America really is a country with a real love of hectic breakfast foods.

TD: A celebration of all-day breakfasts.

BS: I also remember how incredibly cozy it felt sitting in this warm family home right next to the fucking freezing Lake Erie.

JP: Yeah, it was like a block from the frozen lake, right? And it was super frozen, like it was frozen as far as we could see.

LS: That was the thing, because we turned up in the middle of the night. The next morning getting in the van and looking out from the driveway—it was just the lake. It was terrifying. It was just white all the way to the horizon.

BS: The other thing is, I mean, we've turned up to a lot of places in the middle of the night, and turning up to a hotel in the middle of the night is so different to turning up to a warm house.

LS: Yep, totally.

Breakfast at GL's table, Jon (left) and Ben (right). Photo courtesy of The Beths.

BS: Yeah. But turning up and having someone cook you three different and important breakfast foods at one a.m.—

LS: And just to have someone talk to you in a friendly way, in a welcoming way—

BS: To have someone be your dad. Do you have any more details about the food? Tristan . . . there were big chocolate chunks in the pancakes, right?

TD: Yeah.

JP: [*interjects*] There were extras as well, there were a lot of things that you could add to your—

BS: [*interjects*] Yeah! Was there fruit salad?

JP: There was stuff like—

BS: [*interjects*] There was a giant bottle of maple syrup.

TD: And it was the good maple syrup, not the imitation stuff.

BS: There was also a lot of bacon.

TD: There were heaps of bacon. And I just thought that all the food was balanced, you know, didn't need to get out the t-sauce.

BS: Was there coffee?

TD: Felt so well catered for.

BS: Probably was coffee.

GL now shares his memories of that night.

GL: How cool. What a pleasure to be included. Recalling my younger days, and nights, going to a show, enjoying myself, and coming home and making predawn breakfast. To give you all an "at home" kind of experience with Rachel and me serving as your hosts, I thought you'd appreciate some home-style cooking—way better than a chain restaurant for sure! I remember you walking into the house to the smell of just-cooked bacon. I then did just like when my kids were at the table as youngsters, went to it and made traditional GL french toast and pancakes, all topped with Ohio maple syrup. I cook all of it in bacon grease for the best flavor possible. There wasn't a crumb left, big surprise!

It's Time for Tajik Breakfast

by Gus Lobban (Kero Kero Bonito)

I've been fortunate to share some wonderful meals with my friend Gus Lobban, who makes up one-third of the genre-bending British pop group Kero Kero Bonito. I only wish I'd been with him for the breakfast he writes about here—at a twenty-four-hour Tajik café in Moscow.

While I know Gus through his work with KKB—including a somewhat ill-fated co-headline tour with Frankie Cosmos disrupted by the dinnertime burglarizing of their van—his Moscow dispatch comes from a solo DJ gig under his inscrutable alias Kane West. This being a massive all-night rave at a former chocolate factory, the post-show meal coincides with breakfast time for the city's Tajik laborers, and Gus finds himself dining at a restaurant that caters to them. Other observers would cast this as an unlikely collision of worlds, but Gus shows us why it's anything but. *—LP*

June 23, 2017. My day started with the stuffy schlep, undertaken alone, from Bromley South to Heathrow Terminal 4. I'd been booked to DJ under my alias Kane West in Moscow that night, which, through holiday blagging and the resourcefulness of the Russian club community, had turned into a microtour incorporating a show in St. Petersburg the next day.

I'd been to Moscow before with my band, in a culture-shocking twenty-four-hour whirlwind of document stamps and marbled Cyrillic, to open H&M subsidiary Monki's Moscow flagship. However, this would be the first time I'd visit Russia on my own. A mixture of bafflement at the previous trip, my growing traveler snobbery, and a vague awareness of Russia's cultural milieu made me keen to learn more this time around. In the restrictive, oddly specific routine of the international DJ, your only chances of worldly education are within the institutions that enable your employment and basic survival: the airport, the hotel, the club, and the food.

There are several ways dinner can go for a DJ. Often, in a show of slick cronyist hospitality, the promoter will arrange for you to eat at a swish eatery next door or within the venue itself, provided it has a kitchen and a dangerously creative chef. My preferred routine is to scout out a local spot beforehand, dine alone after soundcheck, and roam Shibuya or Huddersfield or wherever I am by night, returning to the venue just in time to walk through the back entrance and straight into the DJ booth. If no one gives a shit, you'll end up with a strange kebab or random green room provisions, like crackers with oranges. There are, of course, drinks and other substances best euphemized "floating around," but through a combination of tourist FOMO (what if I never see Utrecht again?) and monastic professionalism (well, you have to bring something to the table), I never touch these. I'm reliably informed that canal-side frites taste even better and are only slightly less destructive.

My first meal of the trip was in category number one. After barreling through recurrent khrushchyovkas on the Aeroexpress and spotting Chilean football officials (in town for the Confederations Cup) at the hotel, I was picked up by Misha, one of the venue's bookers. With his long navy coat, small round glasses, and genuine fascination with hyperobscure music scenes, Misha occupied the more refined end of the clubbing character spectrum. He drove me to Strelka Bar, my venue for the evening, explaining that it was owned by a Russian billionaire, which meant that Misha et al. pretty much had carte blanche to program whichever bleeding-edge artists they wanted to in the name of novel cultural decadence. Furthermore, I'd be experiencing the summer iteration of Strelka: an outdoor, nightlong party.

We arrived at a scattered complex of buildings, which once comprised a chocolate factory, on an island in the river Moskva, barely a stone's throw from the Kremlin. The Cathedral of Christ the Saviour stood directly on the other side of the water, massive and golden domed. In the middle of the complex was an aircraft-hangar-high open hall fashioned out of what looked like designer scaffolding—the venue. The place was already popping, with large adverts for Martini framing the entrance (brand sponsorship being a handy lifeline for debauchery in Russia and beyond). Misha took me to a bustling rooftop dining space for dinner on the house; I can't remember what I had (my subconscious says duck was involved), but I enjoyed it and it set me up for the night that followed.

Misha was dashing round in true harried promoter style; a Martini representative had let him know that their branding wasn't prominent enough, and that the adverts needed to be moved so more people could see them. While I ate in the unseasonable Moscow breeze, Misha stopped by to run through some details.

"By the way, how long do you want to play?"

"Oh, whatever, I'm easy."

Gus mid-sentence at lunch in London. Photo by Lauren Martin.

"Great! We have you down for three hours, three till six a.m."

I didn't have a DJ agent at this point, and I'd completely forgotten to clarify my own set length before the booking. I wasn't even sure I had three hours of music on my person (I have since learned at least some of the basics of DJ preparation). Still, I let Misha concentrate on advert placement and tried not to worry him further. Sometimes as a DJ it's both more professional and more thrilling to just go with the flow.

My set went well that night. I paced myself and pulled every trick I could think of to fill my slot; fortunately, as Kane West, I was known for a schizoid, experimental approach to DJing, which meant I could get away with playing records like my General MIDI saxophone cover of Burial's "Archangel" and dance tracks in 14/4 time (Strelka was subjected to both). A longer set lets you move between moods in a way you can't over forty-five minutes, and I got to play records I love that I wouldn't normally get the chance to. However, for some reason, I hadn't really anticipated what would happen as I played through morning.

While my Casio house drum tracks rang through the old chocolate factory, the environs lightened gradually, until the Cathedral of Christ the Saviour's dome glistened in the morning sun, its rays bouncing into the river Moskva, and the expanse of a cloudless sky lifted up the whole city. The dancers kept going, some sharing the metropolitan dream with laughing friends, others locked into a psychic tussle with themselves they were determined to finish. Every dance floor is beautiful in a way, but I'm always impressed by the places that don't do it by halves.

I finished with my own "Definitely Come Together," a multi-tempo MIDI prog jam featuring jazz scat singing and a Rage Against the Machine–imitation rap performed by me. We'd made it. The long-haulers clapped and cheered, blinking at the uncannily bright dance floor. Outside was the familiar scene of clubbers vaguely celebratory at having seen the night through, arranging afterparties, taxis home, or a superhuman day at work on no sleep. Among the scattered crowd, I found Misha with Maxim—one of the architects of my band's previous trip to Russia—and their partners. Maxim exclaimed jubilantly, like a tour guide on the first day of a Great Railway Journeys package holiday:

"Now we will go for Tajik breakfast!"

Tajikistan is a landlocked country in central Asia with fewer people than London's urban area and one of the highest poverty rates of any post-Soviet republic, exacerbated by a brutal civil war in the '90s. Though Tajiks are an Iranian people, distinct from the Turkic ethnic groups that predominate in central Asia, Tajik cuisine has much in common with its neighbors, encompassing central Asian stalwarts like pilaf (oily rice with extras, called osh in Tajik), laghman (noodles), and kebabs. However, one dish stands out as distinctly Tajik. Qurutob is really a kind of salad, made by soaking torn fatir (flaky flatbread) in a mild, creamy sauce made by dissolving qurut (balls of sun-dried buttermilk curds) in water. The result is topped with layers of oil, onions, diced tomato, cucumber, and herbs. It's a humble dish in the pantheon of Tajik food, thought to have originated in rugged rural areas, where a little produce needs to go a long way. In Dushanbe's qurutobkhonas, the dish is eaten communally with hands.

While you'd have trouble finding a bowl of qurutob in Bromley, there's a market for it in Russia, which hosts more than a million Tajik workers attracted by the opportunity to generate vital homeward-bound remittances.

With Maxim at the helm, we bundled into a smartphone-summoned cab, which then sidled along the Moskva. Every now and again, one of the Seven Sisters, the stout Stalinist skyscrapers that dot the city, slid past the window bathed in morning sunlight. Through the serene suspension of Saturday-morning Moscow, we ventured beyond the Garden Ring—the circular main road that delineates the very middle of the city—and after about fifteen minutes stopped at a painted concrete hut on a nondescript tree-lined street, opposite a short new-build business development. It felt more like a distant suburb of a Benelux metro area than prime Moscow. This was Cafe Shashlychok-24, a twenty-four-hour (!) eatery offering dishes from across the central Asian spectrum, including, yes, the best qurutob I was likely to find in Moscow.

The only diners inside at six-thirty in the morning, we took a table about halfway down the gray-tiled dining room and were given menus by the T-shirted waiter. There are few more exciting prospects in the modern era than a menu mostly comprising dishes you've never heard of. Alas, it was written in Cyrillic with the odd picture of a triumphant pile of plov or bulging sambusa, so I couldn't read it, but such is the fortune of a well-hosted DJ that I wouldn't have needed to anyway. Maxim ordered two bowls of qurutob with meat—not a component of classic qurutob but offered where available—for the table, and we threw in our own requests. I opted for some buuz, simple meat-filled dumplings associated with Mongolian cuisine, the kind of dish that feels novel to Brits while appealing to the most fundamental aspects of our palate.

When trying unfamiliar cuisines far from home, even the simplest dishes can make you reassess how flavor works. Such was the case with Shashlychok-24's qurutob. The fatir layer was pillowy and moist, infused with the subtle, sour pungency of the qurut. This was a natural match for the salad on top, though the heaps of fried onion and its attendant oil pulled everything in a fiercer, heavier direction than I was used to. The döner-ish slices of meat on top offset the qurutob's potency, helping me acquire its taste and turning the dish into a knockout meal. We ate until we were full, and Maxim generously ordered that any remaining qurutob be doggie-bagged and given to me. My attempts to throw some rubles onto the bill were futile; in any case, the total for five of us came to the equivalent of roughly twenty quid, which seemed fair for a life-affirming culinary revelation.

In many ways, Cafe Shashlychok-24 comes close to defining my ideal eatery—unpretentious, practical, and experienced in delivering flavorful, satisfying food that casually showcases humanity's capacity for the sublime. But I often wonder: What makes Shashlychok-24 so special? Is it an example of how the metropolitan ecosystem unexpectedly supports its disparate fringes, in this case Moscow's all-hours Tajik laborers and its nocturnal youth? In doing what they know well, have the Shashlychok staff hit on the magic that no shareholder-answering franchise could ever come close to? Is it just that middle-class kids like to go on cultural safari?

I would accept arguments for all of these. However, when I get to the heart of it, I realize there is almost nothing better than good food, good company, and good music with a bit of education thrown in somewhere. DJing can be a transient, lonely, and exhausting lifestyle, but when someone tells you that it's time for Tajik breakfast, don't fight it—however badly prepared you are.

Maxim (left) and Gus's bandmate Jamie (right) on a later full-band visit to Shashlychok-24. Photo by Gus Lobban.

Italian Thanksgiving

by Cole Furlow (Dead Gaze; Dent May)

Cole Furlow is a larger-than-life character and one hell of a musician. I can tell you with considerable authority that he is somebody that you want on your team. He brings a lovable, over-the-top flair to just about everything he does, and in the time that we have known each other he has taken very good care of me.

We became fast friends while he was playing bass in Dent May's band when they opened for Real Estate on a summer tour back in 2011. We bonded right away—a pudgy bass players' union in a sea of skinnier, better-dressed guitar players. It did not take me long to figure out that this guy loved to eat as much as I did. Cole is the person who taught me that the best fried chicken in the South usually comes from gas stations. He treated me to fried okra and sweet tea at popular diners, and plate lunches at hole-in-the-wall grocery stores. He once drove hours to pick up three racks of ribs from some roadside pitmaster for an evening of gluttony we lovingly dubbed "Ribgate."

Suffice to say, Cole knows a thing or two about hospitality, and what he captures so perfectly in the essay that follows is just how rare that can be when you're sweating it out on the road as a touring musician. When you do find it, as I did when I met Cole, it can make all the difference. *–AB*

Back in the 2010s, I lived in a show house called the Cats Purring Dude Ranch in Oxford, Mississippi. The Dude Ranch was a thriving scene and a great live-music venue, and we hosted a plethora of the mid-aughts' hottest indie acts. I can say with confidence that we did our best to take care of touring musicians. Gave them couches, food, drink, and conversations, and, of course, we shared our culture of Southern hospitality.

Experience is a wonderful teacher, obviously. In 2013, my band Dead Gaze lucked into a two-and-a-half-week European rock-and-roll tour. I had already been in mainland Europe for a month (touring with another band) before my other bandmates met me in Brussels. I was tired, hungover, and homesick.

One night, we were booked at a club called Moog in Ravenna, Italy. It was Thanksgiving. I'm from the South, so missing Thanksgiving was a big deal. It's probably a big deal for most Americans, but convincing my mother it was worth it to miss Thanksgiving to play guitar in Europe was—for this redneck—a *titanic* deal.

At Moog, a man greeted us at the door, introduced himself, and said, with a thick Italian accent, "I know it's a holiday where you are from, no? Well, we'll give you Italian Thanksgiving tonight!"

Man, did I just hear him say that? Like, he knows? And is actually accommodating, empathizing, and doing something about it? I could've cried, probably did.

We soundchecked, set up merch—we hadn't sold shit on the tour—and settled in for what was seemingly going to be a memorable night. We moseyed upstairs to a loft area, and immediately our eyes met a long white tablecloth–clad, candlelit dinner table with six chairs for the six of us. It was . . . nice. We were so stoked, man. To tell you this was a departure from the two drink tickets we got in Seattle would be a Cooperstown-sized understatement.

They rolled out the food. Family-style everything. Big bowls of freshly rinsed romaine. We had to cut it, which I thought was legit. To honor my efforts to avoid repeatedly using the word *delicious*, I'll just use it once: The salad dressing—albeit simple—was fucking delicious. A subtle, savory lubrication for something green, a food color largely absent on our journey thus far.

Decanters of local vino sat perfect and clean, ready on the table. I was still drinking at that time and had more than my fill. We were disciples of Bacchus, baby! Every sip was a dream. Combined with the salad and fresh, warm bread—we were home. Our teeth were purple like your drunk aunt's.

The main course, like everything else at this joint, was simple, pure, and confident. Homemade fettuccine. Thick and proper, covered in a butter and garlic sauce. Shell-on prawns flanked the noodles, like the ones you don't get where I'm from. That was it! An uncomplicated, from-scratch Italian meal with tried-and-true standbys so satiating they stood on their own.

Our newfound epicurean drummer, Ian Kirkpatrick, was particularly enjoying himself this fine evening. Full of carbs and fermented grapes, he stood up, stretched a bit, and walked to the stairwell. Some time had passed, and we were not paying attention or obsessively gauging the crowd size. "Yo, the bar is packed!" he said from his vantage point at the top of the stairs.

You know that sign that hangs in the tunnel on the way out to the football field at Notre Dame? It says, "Play like a champion today." It might as well have been hanging in that stairwell in Ravenna. We huddled up before we rolled onstage. *The time has come to Rip. Play like a champion today.* We played as hard as we could.

I don't remember everything I said on the mic. I was an over-the-top romantic then, even worse than I am now. I'm sure I said the word *genius* a lot in describing our meal. I do remember I was in the crowd by the third song. A record for that tour by a long shot. That's me at my best! That's me giving it my all. That's me "play[ing] like a champion today." It was because of the food. It was because of the hospitality. Something my home state is arguably known best for. Hospitality. Being fucking hospitable. It goes a long way, and that night was no exception.

I tell y'all all of that to say this: If you take care of a band, the band will take care of you. It's that simple.

My hope for anyone reading this is that if you ever get the chance to be accommodating to a touring band, you won't regret it. Just simply show them the good stuff. The stuff they probably don't have where they're from. They'll reciprocate by showing you their art the way they want you to see it. It might work!

Try to give them your version of my Italian Thanksgiving.

Hospitality at Osheaga. Photo by Susan Moss, courtesy of Evenko.

Promoter Spotlight:
Osheaga Festival

In the backstage area of every music festival you have ever heard of, there is a catering tent. At this catering tent, everyone who is working at the festival, artists and crew members alike, has the chance to come and enjoy heaping provisions from the buffet. It also serves as a veritable lunchroom for the full scope of characters from the indie-rock touring universe—a cosmic way station and high school cafeteria that all bands are bound to encounter at some point along the road.

Crew members, often clad in black T-shirts, donning walkie-talkies, tend to sit together. Some of them might have once toured together with a different band, and you'll hear accents from all over the world yelling hello to one another across a sea of folding tables. Bands tend to sit together too, and it's not uncommon to run into old friends and ex-bandmates here as well. Real Estate tends to occupy middle billing on a typical festival's marquee, and it's usually at catering when we get to catch a glimpse of the headliners in the wild. "Did you see Big Boi at the make-your-own-taco bar?" "Win Butler is really going in on that chocolate cake!" When I first met Carrie Brownstein, it was in the catering tent.

The quality of the food at festival catering tends to be mediocre and limited. Artists are issued "meal tickets" that they have to present before entering the tent, to ensure that the festival is not being ripped off of its precious supply of poached salmon in mustard sauce. The Osheaga Music and Arts Festival in Montreal, however, is a horse of a different color. Long before Luke and I had conceived of this book, I was texting him emphatically from the Osheaga catering tent. Artists are welcome to enjoy as much food as they like, and its superior quality is downright absurd. The year that I got to play (and eat), I pulled an entire lobster directly off a grill and took it back to my table. Festivals' reputations tend to precede them in the artist community—some good, some bad, some just so-so. But touring artists know that Osheaga is a festival you want to play, because at Osheaga, you get to *eat*.

The culinary operation is headed up by two local food personalities, Chuck Hughes (chef/restaurateur) and Danny Smiles (chef), with long histories in the Montreal food scene. Chuck has also had several shows on Food Network Canada, one of which includes backstage footage from an early edition of Osheaga that he told us not to watch. We spoke to them and Nick Farkas, who books the festival with events promoter Evenko, to get the story on Osheaga's legendary catering. *-AB*

Opposite: Pizza from Montreal's Elena backstage at Osheaga.
Photo by Susan Moss, courtesy of Evenko.

Welcome to Artist World

Nick Farkas, Evenko, in conversation with Chuck Hughes and Danny Smiles

The Osheaga Music and Arts Festival
Montreal, Quebec

Chuck Hughes: When I was starting out, I was roadie for a band called Metal Steel, which nobody has heard of, thank fucking god, and a band called Reset that became Simple Plan (back when they were punk). I sold T-shirts and did all the roadie stuff, and then one day they were like, "Dude, can you make your chicken, your famous soya-sauce chicken, you know?" I was twenty-two years old, and that was my claim to fame. That's basically how I started catering backstage . . .

Danny Smiles: I've played in front of like three people in Winnipeg.

Nick Farkas: I think the initial discussion that Chuck and I had was, first of all, tour catering generally sucks. Montreal is the food capital of Canada, and we really wanted to make that statement to the artists who were coming through town: "This is a food city." We wanted that to be a part of the experience.

And food is such an important part of your day. If you start your day off with good coffee and good food, no matter what happens after that, your day is going to be better. You're gonna be nicer to the sound guys; you're gonna be nice to the security people. And you're gonna tell other bands about it.

CH: That's the beauty of Osheaga—it's over 120 bands or something from all over, different walks of life. So our goal was to make this an experience that makes bands wanna come back, and that kind of puts Montreal on the map for them.

DS: I got hired to work as a line cook at one of Chuck's restaurants, and he invited me to the first year [of Osheaga]. I saw what he was doing, and I was like, "I need to fuckin' do this with him—this is music, it's food, it's everything that I love!" That's how it started.

We're not caterers; we have restaurants in the city, so we curate everything backstage as if you're walking into one of the restaurants. These bands are on tour, and maybe they don't have an extra day off in Montreal, so we're trying to give them Montreal in those few hours.

Fresh pasta production at Osheaga's Artist World. Photo by Susan Moss, courtesy of Evenko.

Those two weeks of Osheaga are always when restaurants close down for their summer break, so we get a lot of these cooks that didn't wanna take vacation. We kind of create this army of amazing cooks, and it's almost like a day camp for them.

CH: I don't say we poach people, 'cause they're kinda off at that time anyway, so we're lucky—we get cooks from different really great restaurants. We always come up with a base menu to start off, and then as we go along—kind of like a regular kitchen in a normal restaurant— there are menu changes every day. But we hire the right people, and we kind of harness that instead of saying, "No, stick to the menu." Once the bases are covered, just go wild, and stay on budget, but go wild. And there's this sort of healthy competition between stations to one-up one another.

DS: But we had to stop one guy that had just come back from working at Noma. He was gonna start doing all these siphons, and I was like, "We've gotta cut this guy off now!"

CH: No disrespect, but, you know, there are only so many branches you can put on a plate.

NF: We had a bunch of the Goldenvoice [the production company that runs Coachella] people come over here to check out the festival, and I'll never forget one text going back to California that said, "They have a fucking prosciutto-slicing station!"

When I meet people now and I get introduced, they're like, "Oh, you're the festival with the food!" We hear that every time, everywhere we go.

CH: Bands are always asking us, like, "Excuse me, uh, can I have one of these?" And we're like, "Yeah! Everything here—anything and everything—you can have as many times as you want." And they're like, "Are you serious?" And it's the best day of their life.

NF: I've been to Bonnaroo, I've been to Coachella—we've been all over—and I was blown away: It's an arena caterer preparing all the food from god-knows-where and bringing it in, and you get one fucking meal ticket, and it sucks. It's such a bad experience, especially considering these are festivals that get huge amounts of business.

What makes Osheaga unique is that we've had—how many festivals have come from all over the bloody world to see how these guys do it? We've pushed other festivals to try to up their game. And if that works out for the entire industry, where artists are treated a bit better when it comes to food, then this whole experiment has been valuable on that level.

When you hear bands and crews talk, it's like they're eating out of dumpsters at most festivals in the States. They get to Montreal, and

Pizza from Montreal restaurant Elena backstage at Osheaga.
Photo by Susan Moss, courtesy of Evenko.

Opposite: Osheaga's Artist World catering. Photo by Susan Moss, courtesy of Evenko

they are so friggin' blown away. The bus drivers never leave catering; it's insane. They eat for like a week.

And when you see the guys from the Black Keys and Charles Bradley shucking oysters with Chuck and Danny, you realize that it's a mutual-admiration society, and it's a respect thing. For me to walk back there between sets, running around to grab a slice of pizza or poutine, and I see Charles Bradley standing there with the chefs, I'm like, "Oh my god, my mind is blown." We never could've dreamed that it would end up like that.

DS: Phil Anselmo [of Pantera] was choking us because the vinaigrette was so good. Phil Anselmo walked in and he's like, "Who made the vinaigrette?" We're like, "This guy." He started choking him, and he's like, "Fuck, this is so good!"

CH: That's basically the reason why we do all of this, to get that kind of reaction out of people and to make their day. People have this idea of touring musicians, like U2, that every guy travels in his own plane and has his own chef. And the reality is, it doesn't matter how much money you have or how many people are on your tour. You're still going from city to city, you're in a plane, you're in a car, you're in an airport. The nature of it is grinding, and it doesn't matter who you are—when you get somewhere, it's fun to feel like you're wanted and that you have basically everything that you need.

So that's why we love what we do so much, and that's why we got into cooking—to see a customer enjoy something and come to the kitchen and just say, "Hey, man, that was amazing; thank you so much." That's why we got into food—kind of like why people get into music, so that people can enjoy their music.

DS: We don't get to watch many sets during the festival, 'cause we're there working, but we always catch the headliner. I remember one year it was Slayer, and just going in the mosh pit with all the cooks, after a full fourteen-hour day of cooking. There's this vibe that's, like, the salad guy with the dishwasher . . . who's crowd-surfing! It's the most epic end to any shift. No cooking shift ends with that.

CH: Normally it's a dish pit, but here it's a mosh pit.

Opposite: Danny Smiles (left) with Montreal chef Victor-Alex Petrenko. Photo by Susan Moss, courtesy of Evenko.

Chapter Two

The Brownie Incident: Self-Care and Wellness on the Road

Picture this: It's about one thirty a.m., and I'm finally in bed in a hotel room on the interstate. It's a Courtyard Marriott or a La Quinta Inn or a Best Western; they're all the same. I'm sharing a room with our lead guitarist, who is in bed, lying on his back with his headphones on. He's staring blankly at his phone. We probably look identical, the two of us in bed in this generic hotel room, mouths slightly open, eyelids heavy, scrolling.

I'm not sure what he's doing or what he's looking for on his phone, but I'm on Instagram, obsessively watching fifteen-second clips of the show that we just played. My chief concern is not with how the band sounds; it's with how I look onstage. I'm exhausted from a relentless daily schedule, but I'll do this for an hour or so, watching clips over and over again, zooming in on pixelated blurry blobs so that I can take a good objective look at my own body. In most instances, an hour or so is how much time I'll need to confirm that I am, in fact, *too fat*, and that I should really tighten up my touring fitness routine.

As long as I've been playing shows, people have been taking photos of me onstage, and as long as I can remember, I've struggled with my weight and with compulsive overeating. Back in 2001, future Real Estate bandmates and I started a Strokes cover band to perform at a friend's sweet sixteen. We all went to the thrift store to buy secondhand dress shirts and army jackets, doing our best to impersonate our skinny idols. The show was a resounding success, but when a photo of the band surfaced a week or so later, I spent a significant amount of time on MS Paint trying to crop and edit my belly out of it. This technique did not work.

In the outmoded, imaginary rock-and-roll narrative, musicians are supposed to be "cool," which is all too easy to conflate with being skinny, like the Strokes. But in genres like indie rock, we're not supposed to let on that we care about how we look, so the toll that touring in general can take on one's physical and mental health often goes undiscussed. And on tour, musicians are perpetually photographed, not just by professional photographers and press outlets but also by fans. This can be an extraordinarily challenging dynamic for anyone who struggles with body dysmorphia, disordered eating, or similar issues.

When I start to feel that all-too-familiar body image anxiety sink in on the road, I'll make a series of private resolutions to myself: "I'm not going to drink any beer tonight," or "I'm not going to eat any more green room gummy bears." These resolutions are difficult, if not impossible, for me to keep. The fact of the matter is, touring is frequently uncomfortable. Long drives in the van are uncomfortable, sleeping in a different place every night is uncomfortable, missing your family is uncomfortable. But, to me, *food* is comfortable. This simple fact has led to some of the most memorable meals of my life, but far more often it has led to me gorging myself, zombielike, on bad cherry tomatoes and Stacy's Pita Chips minutes before I perform.

Of course, I'll come offstage feeling heavy and sluggish from two IPAs and too many pita chips, I'll grab a handful of Swedish Fish or mini Krackel bars, then retire to my hotel room where I'll scour the internet looking for hours-old photos of myself. I'll swear to eat healthier the next day, and then I'll repeat the entire cycle again.

This doesn't even take into account the parade of temptation that any traveler must face when driving on the interstate, especially in the US. And while it can be very difficult to eat healthily on tour in the States, it's definitely not difficult to eat *well*. Some of the greatest meals I've had in my life have also been some of the most objectively unhealthy, and many of those have come from hole-in-the-wall roadside eateries. No regrets, baby—but knowing when to go for that extra bacon-wrapped Sonoran hot dog in Tucson, Arizona, and when to hold off is a fine and difficult line that every musician must navigate eventually.

The following stories take a look at how—in contrast to hospitality and care at the hands of *others*—seasoned musicians take care of *themselves* on the road. It's eye-opening, though perhaps unsurprising, that some of the musicians with the most enlightened attitudes toward self-care on tour are also some of those who have enjoyed the most success and longevity in their careers.

To that end, we'll hear from Dawn Richard on reclaiming her relationship to food as a solo artist after years spent in the toxic trenches of mainstream pop. Eric Slick of Dr. Dog regales us with his "Brownie Incident," a cautionary tale of unchecked green room gluttony on his first-ever tour. And Steve Sladkowski of PUP opens up about his struggle with alcoholism and depression, exacerbated by the vodka-friendly foods of his eastern European heritage. That's just a sampling.

As for me, the next time I head out on tour, I'll do it with the intention of striking the perfect balance between physical and mental health. That means knowing when to resist that asada burrito, overstuffed with greasy french fries. But maybe more importantly, it also means knowing exactly when not to. *-AB*

Eating Econo

as told by Bob Mould (Hüsker Dü)

Bob Mould may have created the blueprint for modern DIY touring, but he certainly didn't do it alone. In the early 1980s, his band Hüsker Dü was part of a now-legendary community of like-minded musicians. Along with other totemic icons of the early punk scene like Black Flag, Minutemen, Dead Kennedys, and countless others, Hüsker Dü forged an international network of underground artists who were able to share their music and tour the world outside the limiting confines of the traditional music industry. Most if not all of the bands in this book have been inspired by this formative period, either musically, operationally, or both.

It was a rare thrill to speak with Bob about his unsurprisingly practical approach to food on tour during this fertile time, and throughout his career. What is perhaps most remarkable and heart-warming is how connected he remains to his guiding principles to this day. *–AB*

I grew up in a poverty-line household in a small farming town, raised on home-cooked meals. The idea of going out for food meant going to a drive-in to get a burger or, if you were lucky, a pizza, once or twice a year. Food was home-cooked or came from a school meal program and was for sustenance only; there was nothing at all fancy.

I started working onstage in 1979 with a group called Hüsker Dü, and for a couple of years we pretty much played in the Twin Cities—Minneapolis and St. Paul—which was our home base. My early tour-related food experiences came from hosting other bands rather than the other way around. I used to help with VFW hall gigs and sort of renegade punk-rock shows. There would be bands from the UK that might come through, and, you know, there wasn't a lot of money to be made, but one thing you could do for your fellow musicians was feed them.

We'd get in touch with the bands and ask, "Are you guys vegetarians?" and of course they were all anarcho-punk vegetarians. Then when they would get to town, we'd have a stack of vegetarian sandwiches waiting for them and they'd be terribly grateful; they'd be like, "You know, we came from the UK, and everything in the Midwest has been meat and cheese, so this is really great of you to do this!"

Back then, hosting more popular bands would put you on their radar. They'd have a phone book with connections in it, and if you could prove yourself as reliable, then their managers would see that and be willing to help *you* out. We were all very protective of our phone books. When we started going out on tour, we would be the recipients of that same sort of grassroots generosity from other bands. They'd either make us a big bowl of vegetarian stew or let us know that we should go to the Seventh-day Adventist vegan restaurant a block from the skateboard shop, which was pretty close to the punk-rock record store.

Touring back in the '80s, that's really how all of us survived. Bands would create a network and share this information with one another. Or we'd show up in a town and just look for the skate shop or the indie record store, because experience told us that a place to eat would be nearby. I can remember in the summer of 1981 when Hüsker Dü showed up in San Francisco and were the beneficiaries of the generosity of Jello Biafra [of Dead Kennedys]. He let us sleep on the back porch of his place near Dolores Park with the understanding that we would go down to city hall and get food stamps.

Without the generosity of others, we were left with roadside food, truck-stop food, or whatever vegan places we could find on our own. It might seem kind of extreme to people now, but that was actually how a lot of us operated at the time—getting paid very little money and just relying on the kindness of others (or the California food-stamps program). When I was twenty years old, honestly, I was mostly thinking about where we could get beer and how much money we'd have left over for gas. I think, in order of importance, the things we'd take in would be: alcohol, tobacco, amphetamines, marijuana, and then food. And of course, gas trumped everything.

There was always an emphasis on keeping things "econo," a term coined by our contemporaries Minutemen to describe the way we did things. Just saying the word *econo* is triggering so many memories for me. That saying makes up a lot of our DNA. I remember staying down in [San] Pedro with those guys, and D. Boon [of Minutemen] would get up to make breakfast for everybody. I miss D. terribly. I also remember sleeping under the desks at the old SST [Records] office. Greg Ginn's mom had avocado trees in the backyard, and there were avocados everywhere. It was pretty crazy. I grew up in apple-orchard country, but California, even then, had more raw materials available to make good food.

Eventually, Hüsker Dü put out two records with Warner Bros. that were pretty successful right off the bat. We got up to bigger venues—anywhere from eight-hundred- to three-thousand-sized capacity—and we were eating a little better. When you get to that level, you can submit a rider with basic things on it like a Domino's pizza after the show, a veggie tray, or chips and hot sauce. Those kinds of things are just the basic things, but it was never a big focal point for the band. We kept things so grassroots even as we were selling out theaters. We didn't scale up the catering.

Hüsker Dü wrapped up in January of '88, and after that I made two solo records with a very professional rhythm section that had more specific rider requirements, meal requirements, and even dry-cleaning requirements. For a couple of years, touring went from econo to luxury, but my personal eating habits didn't change that much. My next group, Sugar, which I fronted in the '90s, got really successful really quickly, but we were still traveling econo. We were just asking for the simple stuff on riders, the "chips and dip; pizza after" kind of thing. But back in the early '90s, that's when Subway, the sandwich chain, was really popular and really good.

It's not the same anymore, but thirty years ago Subway was great. It was consistent nationwide, and the bread was always baked fresh on-site. Yeah, the loaves were baked from premade rolls, but so are my favorite Hokkaido cheesecakes at the Westfield mall. It was high quality, it was cheap, and it was consistent. I think psychologically, for me, when I'm on the road, consistency—any kind of consistency—is valuable. Every day is an iteration of the same motif, but things do change from town to town. Back then, you could count on Subway. We could all agree on it, it was fast, and we could eat it on the run. Sometimes when you're touring, those are the things that are most important.

These days, it's all about eating safe as well as eating clean. As I get older, I've got different needs when I'm on tour, and as much as I used to love spicy food or taking chances on more esoteric progressive cuisine, sometimes that doesn't really fit with nine hours in the rental car between Kansas City and Denver. I save my more daring palate for when I'm at home or when I'm in a place for a week, as opposed to being constantly on the go.

Every musician has different times of the day that they like to eat, and for me it's T minus six hours before the show. For me, six hours is great because by the time I get onstage, I'm hungry, I'm light, and I'm ready to go out and sweat about a thousand calories off. It's a really physical show, it's a wet show, and I want to be as light as possible for that. I don't want my body to have to expend any other energy. It's all for the lungs, for the diaphragm, and for the physicality of the show; it's not for digesting a meal I just ate an hour ago.

Afterward I'm really hungry. Every day I put 12 ounces of organic turkey breast on the rider so that I can have a portable meal to take with me when it's three a.m. and I still can't wind down after the show. It's my go-to end-of-the-night meal. Everyone laughs, but I carry my own wraps, so I'm at least guaranteed some protein before I go to bed. I carry condiments, too, as long as they keep at room temperature.

People are always thinking about the Rolling Stones or the brown M&M's or whatever. That kind of mythology, to me, is a whole different world. A lot of what we used to do was 100 percent analog. We were sharing information with trusted allies. These days we're sharing our data with untrustworthy digital companies that mine us so that we can glean that same information. The structure is completely upside down from what I learned.

It's funny, though. I was over in the UK one summer recently doing four weeks of solo touring, and I was traveling with my longtime British tour manager and sound guy. It was just the two of us on the road, and after about a week of being with me, he said, "This is like wartime for you, isn't it? You just eat like it's wartime!" And I said, "Yeah, I guess, pretty much."

Rider-to-Table

as told by Lily Chait, Touring Private Chef to Phoebe Bridgers and boygenius

Lily Chait isn't a musician, but she knows what it's like to go on tour. A serious chef and pop-up specialist, Lily spent time refining the art of simple farm-to-table cooking at Berkeley, California's legendary Chez Panisse. But then Phoebe Bridgers needed someone to cook for her on tour.

Now Lily cooks all over the world for Phoebe and boygenius, but don't mistake her for some kind of hoity-toity private chef. Thrust suddenly into the touring lifestyle—armed with induction burners and miniature ovens shoved into road cases—Lily's culinary style is not just healthy and ingredients-based, it's also kind of . . . punk. *-AB*

The first time I cooked on tour was 2022 for Phoebe Bridgers during all her shows in the US, Canada, and Europe. It was kind of a last-minute thing, honestly. Covid concerns were being taken into account, and the band was also thinking about how long they were going to be away from home. I think we were on the road for three and a half months—it was a long time. That was another reason that they wanted to have me on board, so that everyone—especially the artists—could be eating exactly what was best for their bodies to stay healthy and successfully complete all the shows. Which was a challenge and a feat!

I came in with no idea of what was going on; I am still in awe of the entire operation. My brother is a musician, so I'd heard a little bit about what touring is like, but I had never seen anything on this level before. I was shocked and amazed by everyone's stamina. On tour last summer, we were traveling with three tour buses and three semitrucks—it's huge, huge, huge every day.

In the US and Canada, I was cooking breakfast, lunch, and dinner for the entire band and crew, which was around thirty-five people. On that portion of the tour we had a traveling kitchen that was built into those rock-and-roll-style road cases that we brought around to all the different venues. I didn't really know that much about the equipment beforehand, so figuring out how much power to draw for the traveling oven was always its own hilarious adventure. This kind of setup was new to many of the venues that we were going to. More often it's like, "Paul Simon has a trailer kitchen," or blah blah blah, but this kind of country-chef touring vibe is more unique, I think.

Photo by Lily Chait.

Photo by Lily Chait.

The crew's needs for food are very different from the band's needs for food. The crew is working sixteen-hour days. It's so intense, and they need caloric intake to survive. Finding the right balance on the menu to make everyone happy was kind of difficult, but the main reason I was hired was to keep the band feeling good and healthy. I also prefer to cook cleaner stuff, but it's an intimate responsibility to cook for people on the road. They have control over so little on tour, and to be given food that you're not super stoked on is less than ideal.

Nonetheless, the general vibe of the meals on that tour was, like, yoga-hippie food, which is sort of my vibe, I guess. I try to incorporate some of the flavors of the food of whatever area we're in so that the local crew might be able to source local ingredients to whatever extent they can. If we're in an area that's well known for its barbecue, I'll make something like vegan chili and gluten-free corn bread. I try as much as possible to say, "Local if you have it!" when advancing all of these ingredients for shows, but it's hard to articulate that on my list, which is just one among many, many lists that I'm sure these people are getting.

Sometimes people at the venues who were into cooking would get really excited, and I would get amazing stuff. Other times I would order ten bunches of carrots and get ten bags of baby carrots, so then it would become like a cooking show, trying to figure out what to do with what I've got. There were days when I was really able to prepare food that was in line with my farm-to-table background, and there were other days when I made lunch fully with just a teakettle because that was the only equipment I could use. It was miso soup with wilted vegetables, vermicelli noodle salad, and all of these different herbs and stuff. Phoebe said it was one of her favorite meals.

I made a vegan, gluten-free, mostly-refined-sugar-free dessert every day. I'd make banana cream pie with a date-nut crust and cashew cream or almond-meal chocolate-chip cookies. I made lots of slow-roasted salmon and marinated chicken, lots of braised beans, and *a lot* of leeks. Anytime anyone in the band is cooking a leek now, they send me a picture.

They're all into food, and I think what they do every night is amazing. They put on such a good show. Every night that I had to miss watching at least part of the show, I was bummed. On tour there's always a need to close the book on the day. Seeing the show and feeling its energy is so crucial to being on tour and feeling the meaning of the whole thing. I felt very acknowledged by them for my craft, and it was amazing to experience that kind of mutual appreciation. I can't imagine going on tour with anyone but Phoebe, because I feel like I've been spoiled by how nice and sweet everyone is.

I think part of my intention is to create an environment where anyone can come to the kitchen and hang out and have some space. I'm not a part of the show—you can't get upset with me for some little thing that happened onstage or off, whatever it might be. I'm a separate entity in a way, but I'm also down to hang because I'm just cooking all day. I'm doing my own thing, so I don't feel any kind of social or work-related tension with anyone. I just do my thing and that's it, but I'm providing a service in my own way, which feels nice.

As one of the few people on the crew who isn't actively adding to the show itself, I sometimes get a little introspective and ask myself, "What *am* I doing here?" Then I realize that it's such an essential thing to fuel the artists and their crew in a healthy way. Plus, now I can work a camping stove like no one else you've ever met.

Photo by Lily Chait.

Sweet 16th and the Temporary Lives of Sandwiches and People

by Adam Schatz (Landlady; Japanese Breakfast)

Folks may recognize Adam Schatz as the swashbuckling saxophonist of Japanese Breakfast, the frontperson and songwriter behind Landlady, or a touring multi-instrumentalist from such bands as Man Man, Wye Oak, and Sylvan Esso. But to me, he has been a larger-than-life figure since our youth, when he was the slightly older kid from the other high school who booked all the shows in our hometown. Out of respect to Adam, I will not mention the names of his high school bands here. Except One Eyed Stanley and the Eskapade.

When I first started touring, Adam shared a document with me known simply as "the spreadsheet," a list of musician-vetted restaurants around the US curated by a community of food-focused individuals in bands. In 2019, with the help of our friend Charlie, we turned this into a clunky website called Tour Food that debuted a few months before the pandemic. Bad timing. But we haven't given up on it yet!

Until Tour Food is acquired by Tripadvisor, Adam is left juggling his hectic touring schedule, robust home-sourdough program, and myriad writing projects, which often appear on the website Talkhouse. His trademark and masterful mix of seriousness and levity are on full display in the following piece. *–LP*

I'm awake in Nebraska on a rare day off, my brain is flying half-mast, and I need to eat something. We were in Colorado last night and will be in Minnesota tomorrow. When the state lines were drawn in our country, I don't think anyone planned on people crossing them as quickly or as often as we do in the declining business of rock and roll. But here I am, yesterday's time zone in my rearview and today's breakfast in my crosshairs, and I do what everyone in my position does: I defer to my phone and type in "breakfast sandwich near me."

When Alexander Graham Bell invented the telephone, I don't think he planned on people using it to geolocate the closest stack of eggs, gluten, and etceteras. But when Benjamin Franklin invented the breakfast sandwich, I do think he maybe had a notion that folks would rearrange their whole day to be close to the best one. One day I'll tell you all about when Ben Franklin flew a kite with a ciabatta roll at the end of it, but that's a different story for a different book.

My phone gives me a few disappointing options in the downtown area where our tour bus is parked, one of which presents the image of a man in a pickle outfit dancing out front, either beckoning people inside or daring them to stay away. I ended up not going to Pickleman's Gourmet Cafe (this is real, not like the Ben Franklin thing) and opted to travel much farther for the food that looked much better.

And that's just it. On a day on tour, the food you eat is really the most significant memory you can have. The songs you play might have a tremendous impact on a crowd, but once you've done it twenty-five times in a month, those memories all just kind of blur together. So I go a mile down the road for an egg sandwich that ends up being just okay, and I sit here remembering the memories of breakfast sandwiches past, fondness for their symbolism and their actual construction. And I invite you in.

Allow me to tell you about the One To Go.

Until very recently, on North Sixteenth Street in East Nashville, Tennessee, there was a bakery right on the corner called Sweet 16th, run by a couple of New Englanders who opened the spot in 2004. I ended up there for the first time seven years later, not because I heard it was amazing, but because it was a breakfast sandwich near me. I got the egg casserole on a biscuit sandwich, immediately translated as "One To Go!" by owner Ellen Einstein at the counter, who shouted it back to the kitchen. A few minutes later it showed up wrapped in paper, the kind of hot that your smart brain knows you ought to count to one hundred before eating. But then your idiot hands shove it into your stupid mouth before you count to fifteen, because that's how good it looks.

The taste of One To Go is worth celebrating, but the flavor was equally matched by the price and presentation. A few dollars got you a hot puck rocketed across the counter into your hands so you could move aside and make room for the next person. One To Go was unprecious and exactly what you needed when you got it.

Yes, food can be beautiful and well lit and expertly composed in a manner that would look nice on the internet after being photographed on your phone, but more than anything, food is made to be eaten. And every aesthetic decision that doesn't have anything to do with the act of eating it ultimately interferes with that act. Because the joy felt the moment you eat the great thing is a joy that can't ever be accurately put into words. It's synapse-based. By the time you can even describe it, the specifics of the feeling are gone. And Sweet 16th's One To Go checked every box of what you want out of a "breakfast sandwich near me." Crumbly biscuit, bits of jalapeño lodged in the cheesy egg, portable, and cheap. Not too filling. A bit singular. Just slightly one of a kind. Because I keep remembering it. And I kept going back.

Whenever my band would play in Nashville, a city where many people I love have lived, I'd inevitably be there for only a single day, never enough time to get together with anyone. But on more than one occasion, I'd sound the alarm and on the morning of our departure my minivan of underslept, semishowered musicians would roll up to Sweet 16th to be met by a handful of Nashville friends. We'd all get Ones To Go and hang out for a bit before they'd send us off to Cincinnati or Louisville or Atlanta. It was always a brief but essential convening of jokes and crumbs, these hangs that are seared into my memory, tethered to the sensory joys of the sandwich and the image of my friend who lived in Nashville but no longer does.

When my friend Jessi was diagnosed with cancer, the whole city of Nashville felt it. As a musician, visual artist, and joyous weirdo symbolic of what made the area special, Jessi was important to many. Her band, Those Darlins, is what brought me to town for the first time, to play and eat and crack up. Playing, eating, and cracking up could easily be bulleted as the best parts of being on tour, so write that down in case you give this book to a friend and forget to get it back.

The more I tour, the more I collect people I love in each city, and if I squint from a plane, I can begin to see a map highlighted by these faces. The only other things on the map are foods and record stores, really. As the years of touring piled on, I developed a pride in these beacons that I see as I view the country from above, and I never really considered that any of those lights could go out. But somehow, the brightest one did.

The famous One To Go.
Photo by Adam Schatz.

Jessi got sicker and sicker, and when it became clear that things were quite bad and getting to the baddest point, I flew back to Nashville to be with my people down there as we collectively embarked on the worst kind of waiting. But being devastated around people sharing and understanding the devastation is always better than being devastated alone. Or at least it was then.

So we sat around and we joked and we celebrated a life as it was coming to its unfair conclusion. On the second day of waiting, my friend JT rolled up with a big box in his hand. JT had been the manager of Those Darlins and the first person I met in their universe, when they first visited New York. I would often stay at his house just a few blocks down from Sweet 16th and listen to his records and hear his stories and hear more stories and then maybe hear one of the earlier stories again, and then it was midnight and then he'd order us a miracle pizza. JT liked to provide in that way, and so on this shitty, horrible day he showed up with a box weighing roughly 900 pounds. He had stopped by Sweet 16th on his way to the hospital, and Ellen and her husband, Dan, had loaded him up with complimentary treats, something to take everyone's mind off what everyone's mind couldn't be taken off of. We marveled at their kindness and then shoved brownies into our sad faces, adding a fond asterisk to a memory of devastation.

What I didn't know at the time was that Dan Einstein of Sweet 16th went to the mat with cancer himself in 2012, and ten years later the cancer forcefully returned. I ended up back in town in front of Ellen at her bakery counter not long after Dan had died, knowing I didn't truly know her and that there's not much to say when someone has lost so much. So I asked for One To Go and took a magic piece of what they'd built together out the door.

Just six months later, I saw the news that Sweet 16th would be closing. Ellen was grateful for the community support but didn't want to continue the bakery without Dan at her side. And whenever I went in, he was always at her side, running back into the kitchen, Red Sox cap framing his smiling face. The bakery was set to close on October 29, my birthday. Cosmic, perhaps. I picked the wrong day to quit sniffing astrological glue, because horribly I had no plans or abilities to be back in Tennessee before that date.

I wrote to numerous loved ones in town to see if they could maybe grab One To Go for me and freeze it. Maybe I knew I'd be writing a piece like this, and I imagined a clean conclusion with my nose pressed against a toaster oven glass as the holy sandwich defrosted, noticing an ancient rune in one of the ridges of the biscuit that would allow me bring the dead back to life. But as usual, reality stepped in.

The sad fact was that the demand for "breakfast sandwiches not near me" that final week was extreme. Anytime my pals went to check, there'd be a line out the door, down the block, everyone hoping for one last One To Go before it went for good.

And so my plans were dashed, but I think that's okay. The One To Go can persist as an intention, a flag to fly for the necessary sharing of personal joys before everyone gets back on the road again to sing their songs or sell their memes door-to-door or whatever people do in the future when you, the reader, are reading this.

They say it's not about the destination, it's about the journey, but I think that's bullshit. The sandwich is much better when you eat it at the destination. It's hotter that way. Some would say too hot. So this is a celebration of a destination gone to pasture and the gatherings it made possible.

I may never eat One To Go again, but I'm at peace with that—the best thing at this point is to just let it live on in my memory. What could be nearer to me than that?

The Conductive Diet

as told by Kaitlyn Aurelia Smith (KAS)

Kaitlyn Aurelia Smith (KAS) likes to read books about Olympians.
This might not be surprising if you've ever met her. On tour, as in life,
she pursues her goals with the regimented precision of a world-class
athlete. She's also down to earth, highly relatable, and a lot of fun
to be around. I'm speaking from personal experience here—KAS is
an old friend of mine. She is the sole practitioner of her own holistic
approach, which includes a daily yoga routine and mind-bending yet
emotionally available electronic music composition.

   When we caught up with her, she gave new meaning to one of the
central theses of this anthology, which is that the food musicians eat
on tour has a direct effect on the shows that they play. *-AB*

I love feeling good! My body feeling good is crucial for my
creativity—but "good" has been something I have worked to
define for myself over the past decade, and I'm constantly open
to evolving and learning more about what I need to feel good.
At the moment, it means making sure my body and mind feel
well enough and calm enough to make decisions I trust.

   Of course, I don't always have the luxury to put off work or life
until I feel good enough to do something, but I try my best to take
care of myself by spending time focusing on finessing how I feel
each day. Touring always creates obstacles for me. When I first
started touring, I had such a rubber band feeling of adrenaline,
come down, adrenaline, come down—night after night. That
can do a lot to the body. It was always hard to sleep after playing
a show, and travel call times the next day would be so early that
sleep deprivation was a real struggle. I had to find new techniques
that would help me feel good on tour, and the biggest things that
help are how and what I'm eating.

Photo by Aubrey Trinnaman.

Before I create, I have to understand where my nervous system, head, and flow are at for the day, and I've noticed that certain foods really interfere with that. I realized I had three parameters for food while on tour:

1. I need food that fills me up enough but not too much so my mind can stay sharp. I like to multitask a lot while performing and I need my brain to be agile.

2. The food needs to be easily accessible, even at an airport or train station.

3. I'm a solo artist and I like to travel light, so I choose foods that are easy to carry everywhere.

At one point I decided to make my own protein shakes on tour and started to carry a travel blender with me, but that didn't last very long. At this juncture I'd been touring for a long time and I was excited to have finally earned enough airline status to use the Delta lounge. The first time I went in there, I looked ridiculous. I was carrying my synth under a rain protector strapped to my stomach and I had my backpack on my back. I sat down with this portable smoothie blender that I hadn't tried yet, and poured in all these ingredients: avocados, protein powder, coconut, and all these other gooey, gross things. I turned it on and everything just exploded all over these very serious-looking people in suits. I completely lost it. I felt so bad but I couldn't stop laughing while trying to pat people down with napkins. End of the travel blender phase.

I use a conductive-touch capacitance keyboard called the Buchla Music Easel, and because food is also conductive, my diet can literally affect the way that the keyboard behaves. This has been really fascinating to learn. I finally homed in on what foods I have to eat to keep my electricity at the right level for each show.

I started doing research on impedance levels and I learned that, just like with an audio signal, if you have a lot of electricity flowing through you, you want to have high impedance in your body so that it can be navigated in a steady way. The amplification process adds so much electricity to a live performance, and so does bio-electricity. When you're in front of people, you have to factor in their electricity too—it's a very kinetic process. I've looked into the impedance levels of fats, minerals, protein, and glucose, and from what I've read, fats have a high impedance and fructose has a low impedance.

I've figured out the right combination of foods to eat when I'm performing. For me, it's something green in the morning, like cucumber or celery, for the conductive minerals. Then I need a high impedance food, like chia seeds and peanut butter. I also like to add shaved ginger and lime. A huge bowl of this fills me up enough that I don't need to eat until after the show—I play best when I'm not feeling sluggish. After playing, I eat tons of fresh fruit and everything else on my rider, except what I need for the next morning. I repeat this every day except for days off.

All that being said, I wouldn't really recommend eating like this to someone else. Everyone is different. I personally think it's really fun experimenting with how I prep for a performance—listening and responding to my body—sort of like how an athlete preps. After tour, I'm eating differently; I love cooking and I love sharing meals with people—I'm not so concerned about my conductivity levels at home.

Figuring out what my body needs in certain situations has really helped me, and I feel like eating the way I have on tour has improved my performance. In addition to my diet, I've found another solution for the rubber band feeling. It's probably such an obvious solution to most, but I learned that I really needed to complete the conductive circle before going to bed. I need a hug after playing, and I need to see a picture of the show so I know it happened.

Tour Diary, May 28–June 3, 2021

by Hermon Mehari

Hermon Mehari, the Kansas City-born trumpeter living in Paris, performs both his own music and in groups—often working in jazz and jazz-adjacent realms but occasionally drifting into the world of indie rock. An obsessive food lover, Hermon's tours are often what he refers to as "touch and go," meaning he'll sometimes perform with several different groups in different cities in the span of a week. He documented one such week of shows (and their corresponding meals) for us in the late spring of 2021.

Those who find resonance with Hermon's inner dialogue would do well to heed his example, whether traveling for business or pleasure. And if you see him rushing across a European train station clutching a bag of takeaway, take note of where it's from. It's probably delicious. *–LP*

Paris–Bourges

Friday, May 28, 2021

My alarm across the room startles me awake. Six a.m. Like most nights before the start of a tour, anticipation robbed me of a good night's sleep. But there's a train to catch.

Outside my window, the sun is just barely rising over my quiet and mostly empty Parisian street. I built in just enough time for an AeroPress coffee and a quick shower. And, of course, when I say just enough time, I mean just enough time to route myself an extra twenty minutes out of the way to stop by Du Pain et des Idées for my favorite croissant. I grab my trumpet and backpack and head out.

As I approach the famed bakery, the smell of butter a block away already confirms that I made the right decision. What better way to both begin a day and leave Paris? Buttery, flaky, dense in the middle, and with a unique touch of sweetness in the dough, these croissants are unlike any others in the world. Something about that makes the moment even more worth it.

At this point, I'm rushing to catch my train, all the while telling myself that I have no regrets. I find my train to Bourges and the other members of the group sitting in the train car. It's a small orchestra led by Uèle Lamore working with a band and some well-known singers in France, including Lou Doillon and Sandra Nkaké. We're putting on a Portishead tribute commissioned by a big festival. I pass out croissants to the musicians nearest me and they are blown away. An American in Paris has shown them the best croissants they've ever had. I'm actually quite used to this reaction by now—most Parisians will go to the bakery nearest them, which, to be fair, is quite easy, as Paris is full of bakeries.

Bourges is a small town with a beautiful medieval center located just two hours south of Paris. Its centerpiece is one of the most famous cathedrals in France, where we happen to be playing. As we arrive, I immediately start eyeing the green room offerings while everyone else marvels at the cathedral. I have one thing in mind—lunch. This region is known for pâté aux pommes de terre, which is essentially a potato pie. I've never had one, and it's my top priority. I glance at the schedule and, calculating how long it takes for things to get set up, I head out into the town in search of one.

I end up asking locals where I can find one. Most smile and recommend the same place. I start to get my bearings around the incredibly well-preserved ancient center of town and finally find the pâté aux pommes de terre. It's fine. Nothing special. But I'm overwhelmingly content. It's hard to describe why . . . but it's both the pleasure of crossing a nagging desire off my list and experiencing the hyperlocal culture of this place. I'm so caught up in the food that I almost take our concert—in a magnificent cathedral—for granted.

We have a great show and everyone is thrilled. It ends rather late, so we have to go eat dinner at the catering service provided for musicians because in France, especially outside of Paris, most places close relatively early. The meal is disappointing, which is to be expected. As much as I try to make every meal count, I'm used to catering meals at this point and don't let it dampen my spirit.

Bourges–Paris–La Ferté-sous-Jouarre

Saturday, May 29, 2021

I'm on the train to Paris, and I go over my route for the third time in my head. I will have one hour to catch my train to La Ferté-sous-Jouarre from a different station. The plan is to make a detour through the Belleville neighborhood to grab my favorite banh mi for lunch. I hesitate and consider just taking it easy and grabbing a sandwich at the train station. It's safe, no stress, and I could find something decent. But I keep thinking about the marriage of the baguette, the grilled chicken, lemongrass, carrots, pepper, and sauces. Decision made. I head to Saigon Sandwich.

I'm panting as I board my train and take my seat. A bead of sweat trickles down my forehead. One bite into my sandwich is all I need to tell myself the trouble was worth it. Is that it? Is this my antidote to all the constant travel? The early mornings, long waits at airports, hectic transfers, delays, long train rides, car rides, flights . . . Certainly the musical part is what it's all for, but something about eating a satisfying meal unique to the place I'm in really makes it all click.

This time I'm playing with singer and bassist Sélène Saint-Aimé at a festival in a rural area on the edge of the Île-de-France. After the show I head back to the catering area because I have only one hour before I catch my train to Paris. Even more disappointing than the night before. There was a time in my life where this would have really annoyed me. But I understand now that there are limits to what's possible—and of course, how ridiculous it is to constantly have expectations beyond that. Or maybe I'm just all right with it because I'm going to Italy tomorrow.

Paris–Bolzano

Sunday, May 30, 2021

After a very early flight and only a few hours of sleep, I arrive at the Milan airport. Due to the coordination of other pickups, they have me arrive a few hours before my festival shuttle service. Normally this would be a reason to complain, but in this case, it means I can go eat in the city. Italy is the country I know best in Europe, and Italian cuisine is my absolute favorite on the continent. I imagine most people who've been to Italy feel this way. There's a certain calm I feel here that I know is linked to the fact that you don't have to try very hard to get a great meal.

When in northern Italy, you eat risotto. And in Milan you eat risotto alla Milanese, which is made with saffron, giving the dish its particular golden hue. I've been working on my own recipe for a while, so I'm particularly excited to eat it in situ today. I find what I'm looking for at Antica Trattoria della Pesa, a place I haven't been in a few years. I savor each bite and find that my own recipe is not too far off. This, too, seems to be another dimension of the importance I place on eating while traveling—it informs my

Hermon with cacio e pepe in Italy. Photo courtesy of Hermon Mehari.

own cooking, which pays everlasting dividends. Or maybe I'm just trying to convince myself my obsession is not too ridiculous.

A four-hour van ride later, I find myself nestled between the Dolomites in the town of Bolzano. This region is right by the Austrian border, and they speak more German than Italian. Clearly the food culture is different here too. I used my time in the van to do research, so I know exactly what I'm looking for: stinco di maiale. Ham hock braised in beer.

I do a soundcheck with the band, the Michelangelo Scandroglio Group, which is a modern jazz group of great Italian musicians whom I am very close to. I find Italians to be very into their food culture, so it's always a blast being surrounded by them. They confirm my suspicions—the stinco di maiale is the thing to get, and we end up at a restaurant that specializes in it for dinner.

Bolzano–Paris

Monday, May 31, 2021

Strudel di mele (apple strudel) and an espresso for breakfast. I follow that with my other tour pastime—running. As I run along the Adige River, I admire the beautiful mountains on either side of me and think about how I wouldn't have been able to see some of these vistas if I hadn't gone for a run. I feel the same way about food. Just digging a little bit further into culture through eating makes the short experience feel more worthwhile.

We have an unusually early performance, at noon, followed by a quick lunch of a simple but delicious panini with speck, and I hurry to catch my van back to Milan. I have time in the airport only for a margherita pizza, but it's a decent Italian chain that I know and ends up being a satisfying end to my short Italy trip.

Paris–Istanbul

Tuesday, June 1, 2021

After a late-night arrival in Paris, I get up early for a video shoot with Sélène Saint-Aimé's band. Before heading to the beautiful theater in the heart of the 9th arrondissement, I make my way quickly by the boulangerie Mamiche for a pain au chocolat. The folds on the pastry are immaculate and the chocolate in the middle bursting with flavor. French breakfasts are the most simple, delicious ways to start a day.

Luckily the recording goes by smoothly and quickly, because I have to head to the airport for a flight to Istanbul. One benefit of packing light is that I'm more mobile—and can be flexible when I need to go out of my way to get food. This time it's the famous falafel sandwich from L'As du Fallafel. This is a place I discovered my first time in Paris, over ten years ago, and it has many memories attached to it. In a city that doesn't have many options that are convenient, inexpensive, *and* delicious, L'As du Fallafel is a gem. I board my plane full and content.

After a few delays, I am finally on the bus into Istanbul. I'm getting in rather late to have a sit-down meal at a restaurant, but I'm not deterred. Unlike Paris, Istanbul excels in this situation. And I know exactly where I'm going: Dürümzade. In fact, I make sure to go here at least once on every visit to Istanbul. As the name suggests, their specialty is dürüm—a simple wrap filled with döner kebab. And it's one of my favorite things in the world. I even turned some of my Turkish friends on to this place, and they can't stop going! I found out about it several years ago while watching the Istanbul episode of *Parts Unknown*. If there's anyone who makes me feel less ridiculous about my food obsession, it's Bourdain.

Istanbul–Bursa–Istanbul

Wednesday, June 2, 2021

After my first decent night of sleep in almost a week, I head to get a Turkish breakfast. This is quite the opposite of a petit déjeuner. It involves a big spread of cheeses, jams, honey, tomatoes, olives, simit, menemen, sucuk, kaymak, and more. I have a Turkish coffee and run to the meetup point for the band.

I get in the van with the other members of the Jef Giansily Quintet, whom I play with most often when in Turkey. We catch up a bit and start talking about what we will eat in Bursa when we arrive. Turkish hospitality is such that the festival asks us to share our location through WhatsApp so the restaurant can follow us and be ready with our orders!

The thing to eat in Bursa is iskender kebab. I've had good iskender in Istanbul, but this is the city it hails from and I'm excited because it's my first time here. The dish consists of thinly sliced döner kebab with a tomato-butter sauce and extra butter drizzled straight from the frying pan, all sitting on a bed of toasted pide, which absorbs the juice from the meat and butter. And you mix all of this with Turkish yogurt—which, in all its full-flavored richness, I have to add, is nothing like the kind of yogurt most people are used to in the States. The combination of these flavors blows me away every time, and finally enjoying an iskender kebab in its city of origin is, unsurprisingly, a delight. How am I supposed to soundcheck after this?

The evening show at the festival goes well, and by the time it's over we're all somehow hungry again. This festival feeds us with style. They arrange a series of mezes for us, which is a welcome break from all the meat. I wash it down with the others by having raki, the anise-scented national drink, before we all have to return to Istanbul.

Opposite: Turkish breakfast in Ayvalık. Photo by Hermon Mehari.

Istanbul–Paris

Thursday, June 3, 2021

An early-morning flight but it doesn't matter. I wake up even earlier than necessary to take a cab to Karaköy Güllüoğlu for the best baklava in Istanbul. I could use the extra sleep, as I have my album-release concert this evening, but in the end, I can't resist the temptation. Plus, at this point, my friends in Paris almost expect me to bring back a box of baklava each time I return from Istanbul.

While on the plane, I reflect on the intense week I've had. Touring is usually made up of hours and hours of travel with a sixty-to-seventy-five-minute show stuck in the middle. And when it's what I call "touch-and-go" touring, it can be an endless string of days like this. After you add in the load-ins, the soundchecks, any extra rehearsals, and other miscellaneous things, it can be quite exhausting. And as incredible as touring can be for seeing places and parts of the world, it is most definitely not a vacation.

I honestly don't know how well I would have enjoyed this past week without those food experiences. They give me something else to look forward to and a way to connect to the place that I'm in so briefly. When I'm onstage, I don't feel like I'm playing to a random crowd. I have a deeper sense of where I am.

Opposite: Pistachio kebab in Antalya. Photo by Hermon Mehari.

REST STOP: THE UK

The dining room at Tebay Services.
Photo by Luke Pyenson.

JC Cairns (Martha)
In Conversation with
Ruby Tandoh

When most American bands tour overseas for the first time, their first stop is the United Kingdom. And there's nothing American bands love to talk about more—other than the Dover-Calais ferry—than the overwhelming superiority of UK service stations over the sad US counterparts we call "rest stops." It's not just prawn cocktail–flavored chips that beguile us: It's the kaleidoscopic variety of sandwiches and salads at Marks & Spencer; the ubiquitous availability of hot, crunchy sausage rolls; and the sense that roadside food there is not just an afterthought.

But that's our view; a true deep dive into British service stations needs British guides. So in order to tackle this important topic, we got in touch with Jc Cairns, guitarist of Durham-based DIY stalwarts Martha. Jc was described to me by a mutual friend as "king of the servos," and it's easy to see why this might be appropriate: He drives and tour-manages other bands when he's not on tour with his own. He spends *a lot* of time on the motorway.

That same mutual friend put us in touch with the wonderful British food writer and cookbook author Ruby Tandoh, who'd recently written a column for the British food newsletter *Vittles* about *"incidental eating"*—exactly what goes on at service stations. Her inclusive, thoughtful approach seemed tailor-made for this subject. Her familiarity with the British DIY scene is just icing on the proverbial cake.

It's only kind of hyperbole to say that I wish the following conversation could've gone on forever—such is my passion for UK services. For everyone's benefit we reluctantly condensed and edited it. *–LP*

Jc Cairns: I really see service stations as these in-between, liminal places that are for some reason completely teeming with life. At service stations, you get an amplified version of British culture, so you've got your Greggs, you've got your WHSmith, and then everybody in amongst it. Everybody's stoked to get a Costa latte. I mean, my dad used to take me to the service station across the road as, like, an evening out. "Let's go to Birtley Services; we'll get the new issue of *The Beano*!" You know?

Ruby Tandoh: I'm delighted to hear this.

JC: My dad would work late, and it was just something to do—it'd be a ride out in the car, so we'd go. They're always open, and, you know, this country does *stop*, but service stations don't. There's always a light on.

RT: That reminds me of something that I heard about—I'm sure you know all about this—but Watford Gap Services used to be called the Blue Boar, and it became a real hub in the '60s and '70s. It was one of the earlier motorway service areas, and especially at the time—this is still true today, as you were saying—the UK is not a twenty-four-hour culture, so it was one of the few places that you could always count on being open.

Salads at Marks & Spencer. Photo by Luke Pyenson.

And so outside of London in the '60s and '70s, the Blue Boar was *the* poppin' place—like, that's where everything was going on—and it became this real musical hub. You had *everyone* going there: There's all kinds of stories about the Rolling Stones being there, Tom Jones was there, I think Jimi Hendrix went through there, and I find it absolutely wild that that's *Watford Gap*, one of the most boring places on earth, to our imaginations. And I can see why that happened in the absence of a consistent nightlife or twenty-four-hour diners. Why these road spots would kind of glow in the dark and, like moths to a flame, people would end up gravitating toward them.

JC: Yeah, and I really feel like that's still the case now—maybe not anything as glamorous as the Blue Boar, but there are times when you find yourself on tour at the motorway service station Travelodge or Days Inn or whatever, and what else do you do? You go and hang out at the service station.

RT: It touched me what you said about—I think the words you used were, you said they're "teeming with life," which is actually a really lovely way to put it. They're very predictable in their way, like in terms of the setup, which is partly because of the bureaucracy: The service area has to be a designated thing; you can't just put a restaurant by the side of the motorway and call it a motorway service area. They have to be open twenty-four seven, they're not allowed to serve booze, they have to be run by an operator, and I think for those reasons there isn't really any kind of organic food culture that flourishes in these places. They have to be chains, and they end up being really formulaic. And so the idea that even though they're so predictable in that way, that life still flourishes—I like that; I'm touched by it.

JC: Yeah, but at the same time, because there is kind of like a blueprint for motorway services, you know, you go there and they try and shoehorn you into a transactional relationship. It's like, you show up, you buy your cup of tea, and then you're outta there. But it's not the case. Life finds a way.

Both: [*laughing*]

RT: That is a *stunning* way to put it. I love that: against overwhelming odds.

JC: Do you have a favorite services?

RT: I mean, I'm not familiar enough with the services to have a favorite one, but I did once get stranded on the M4 at Chieveley Services. I broke down, so I had to stay at the Travelodge there, which was genuinely one of the most fun experiences of my life. I just love the nothingness of it. But yeah, I would assume at this point that you have a pretty comprehensive mental map of all the services out there. Like a hunter-gatherer who knows where all the best berry bushes are.

JC: Yeah, and the best thing is when a new one opens.

RT: *Interesting.* How often is this happening?

JC: I think maybe once every five years.

RT: [*laughing*]

JC: It's not a big country. And do we need any more services? But anytime a new one opens, everyone gets excited about it. There's a new one outside Leeds, and I feel like that's a *hot* day-out destination.

RT: Whereabouts outside Leeds?

JC: It's called Skelton Lake [*laughing*]. It's got a lake, so, you know, it's got a bit of "nature." And it's got a Nando's.

RT: A Nando's?! That *is* exciting; I'm not even bullshitting when I say it: I've not seen that in a services before, and that's genuinely exciting.

JC: I think it's worth saying for folks who don't know: Nando's is a chain of chicken restaurants, but it's a night out, or it's part of a night out. To kind of throw that into a space that it wouldn't normally be in— throw a Nando's in there, and there's a reason to go! There's another service station on the M25, I can never remember what it's called, but there's a Wetherspoons in there.

RT: I thought you were not legally allowed to have anywhere selling alcohol in a services!

JC: [*laughing*] Wetherspoons have managed to bend those rules, so there's a full Wetherspoons open in a service station. It seems like a horrible idea, but here we are.

RT: I'm really interested in this idea: What you said about the Nando's, that genuinely kind of excited something in me, and—I know the feeling of driving along, and you see the McDonald's arches on a motorway services, or you see it on a sign—you see something that feels a little bit like an old friend, seems a little bit like a feature on someone that you recognize. And it's just Burger King, or it's just the sign for an M&S, but the recognition of the brand in that moment must feel quite comforting in a way.

JC: It's the familiarity, you know? Especially when you're in between states, in between places, and there's something holding its arms out—I guess that's why they do it, but you're right: There is comfort there.

RT: Do you crave that familiarity?

JC: This is probably an unpopular opinion to have, but I would take a chain restaurant any day of the week. On a rock-and-roll tour, there's so much uncertainty there; anything can happen in between those shows, in between those cities. And then when there's something there that you recognize, you know what you're gonna get, you know it's there for you, I'm like, "Yeah, gimme Nando's over this unknown that might be awful," you know? And that might just be me, but—

RT: I can relate to that.

JC: They do know what they're doing.

RT: So let's say for example you're driving an American band around the UK. Where do they most want to go?

JC: Most American bands come to me with a wish list. And at the top of that wish list is Tebay Services. [*laughing*]

Posh sandwiches at Tebay Services. Photo by Luke Pyenson.

RT: *Not* Tebay again; I hate hearing about Tebay!

JC: It's *always* Tebay. It's sometimes, "Ah, what's the rest stop with the ducks?" and I'm like, "It's Tebay."

RT: [*laughing*]

JC: And, you know, usually you end up there so far into a tour. You've done the Greggs, you've done the Watford Gap, you've done all of that, and then you show up at Tebay. And non-European bands are like, "What is this magical place?" But my feelings about Tebay are different because, yeah, I've been there, I've done it. Honestly: It ain't my place. I don't belong.

RT: Explain, for the sake of anyone who hasn't had the luxury of going to Tebay, what goes on there and why it's so different.

JC: Tebay is an independent service station that was put together by farmers in the Lake District to make the most of this almost captive audience they had passing through. So it's a little more highbrow—you haven't got your big brands, there's not a McDonald's there, there's not a Costa Coffee, there's not a Starbucks. It's all locally produced and organic. The food that you get there is real food. You see it being cooked in front of you.

On a tour where hot meals are sometimes hard to come by—and I had a drummer in the van a few months ago who was like, "A hot meal makes or breaks a day"—if you get a hot meal, you're gonna have a good day and you're gonna have a good show. Some days you're eating crisps and hummus in the van, and sometimes that lasts for days on end. I once did a tour—this was in the US—where we stopped at a cinema, and we got unlimited popcorn—about six of us. We took that with us, and we ate popcorn for about three days. That was how we lived.

RT: Miserable. Absolutely miserable.

JC: I couldn't do that now, but the hot meal is important. And I think that's why Tebay is so popular with touring bands. Also, it's out in the countryside, which is pretty beautiful at the right time of year. I do always like taking people there because they get something out of it; it feels like a landmark.

The class element is the only thing, to me. I mean, I very much feel like I don't belong among the people who go there. The clientele is a very particular brand, you know? And a van full of dusty punks climbing out does not really go over very well. Like, it's almost a very middle-class clubhouse on the M6 motorway. And it's also—as service stations go—it can be kind of expensive, like almost prohibitively so. Not everybody riding the motorways of the United Kingdom has twelve pounds to spend on, I don't know, a fuckin' scone! Sometimes people are like, "Ah, fuck, I've been driving for five hours, and I've got two quid. I need a fuckin' sausage roll!" That isn't possible at Tebay. And you know, everybody uses a service station for the same reasons: wees, poos, and sausage rolls.

RT: Is that Maslow's hierarchy of needs? [*laughing*]

I was just gonna ask—in terms of when you do go to a service station where you feel at home, where you feel like you know the language of the place, the rhythms of the place—when you're there and either you're touring yourself or you're driving a band, whom are you running up alongside? 'Cause sometimes you go to a service station, you have something to eat and drink, you drive for six hours, go to another service station, and you can actually find yourself in there at the same time as people you were in the first one with, just purely by accident. So who are the other people? You've got bands on tour; who else do you find coming into this kind of temporary community?

JC: Obviously you get your truckers. And maybe they're the kings of those places; I don't know. But then, you know, there's the family holidays—they started their journey to Devon at three a.m., and it's six a.m. now, and they've stopped for a sausage roll. So everyone's in their dressing gowns [*both laughing*], and they're inhabiting the same space as, like, the business pricks. You know, with their briefcases and *their* sausage rolls. [*laughing*] Everyone's there for their sausage rolls!

It is kind of special when you bump into other touring bands in service stations, 'cause there's the kind of knowing camaraderie. It's like, "Yep, we're on the same circuit here." But it's cool: There aren't many places where you can get a family of five all dressed in their bathrobes and, I don't know, like, a pharmaceutical salesman . . .

RT: It feels like the start of a joke, like, "A family of five in their bathrobes, a pharmaceutical salesman, and a metal band walk into a service station . . ."

I think that's beautiful. It's a great leveler in a way. Everybody is hostage to the same selection of places to eat, which are comforting and good and cheap in some ways, and also sometimes uninspiring in other ways. But everybody there is on the same level.

JC: You're using words like *hostage*—I'm not having negative feelings about any of these! Because we're all just feeling these same things, and we're all just here together.

You know: Ain't that just a lot like life?

Both: [*laughing*]

Opposite: Lamb stew, chunky chips, cabbage, and peas at Tebay Services.
Photo by Luke Pyenson.

Tapas Alone

as told by Natalie Mering (Weyes Blood)

When you stick around in a particular music scene long enough, you might get the opportunity to witness an artist's full stratospheric trajectory, as I have with Weyes Blood. When I first met Natalie, she was probably nineteen years old, living in Philadelphia, and making challenging esoteric music that can only be described as "noise-folk." Fans of her most recent albums might be surprised by her early experimentations, but even then she had a reputation among a certain crowd for being at the top of her own class.

It's common when an artist transcends humble origins and achieves wider popularity for them to experience a kind of wistful nostalgia for "the early days." Success can usher in so much change for a musician, and often what changes first is the way they eat on tour. We had a conversation with Natalie in which she told us two stories of eating alone at both the beginning of and more recently in her career—two ends of the spectrum. On the surface so much seems to have changed for her, but has it really? *-AB*

I feel like if somebody else had been with me, they would've been like, "Don't eat that!" I had seafood bisque on an overnight train from Spain to Portugal. I was so enchanted by the idea of a dining car that was open all night, so I just waltzed in and had a little glass of wine and was like, "Oooooh, a seafood bisque!" That was the cheapest thing on the menu, and I just got slammed. I mean this was some historic food poisoning—I didn't feel the same for, like, four months.

I was on tour promoting this record called *The Outside Room* on a small LA label called Not Not Fun. It was definitely a noisy album and a noisy set, where I would play really loud, crazy distorted music—they were still my folky songs, but through the guise of tape noise and weird stuff and keyboard. This was 2010. I had a Eurail pass and I was carrying all my bags, traveling from place to place.

I booked that tour myself and I remember in all my emails to promoters saying, "You need to feed me!" So I did get some really exciting hospitality because it was so DIY. People would treat me and take me out, and that's something that's become a little more rare as I've gotten bigger. I might get a promoter every once in a while who wants to show me what's up, but most people assume I don't want to book a dinner with a stranger. Most of the time when it comes to feeding myself, I'm eating catering or I'm on my own.

I was a solo artist before I had a band, so when I got my first band I was like, "Let's all hang out all the time!" Maybe it's my Christian upbringing—I felt like if we all bonded during dinner, then we'd all bond onstage. I feel that food is culture and connection, so while I do enjoy a solo journey, for me, a meal is all about people being together.

But when it's your band, when it's not like a *band*-band where everyone's an equal part—if you're the boss—people don't always wanna be buddy-buddy to the degree of eating daily meals together. There's this ominous air around asking bandmates to a meal, maybe the fear that you could fire or reprimand them. And—not like I was ever a crazy diva—but when I became more of a *thing*, the dynamic just really shifted. I started hiring people who were more like hired guns who had done a lot of tours, maybe they'd had certain experiences with different bosses—I'm not saying that they didn't want to hang out, but it was different from the DIY "we're all in it together" kind of feeling. They needed independence.

It's funny how it works, and there are always exceptions, but at a certain point, when your band starts to get bigger, the pressure increases and each bandmate may need to strike out on their own, like, "I just need to go take this walk and have a miso soup solo somewhere." I come from underground music, so I'm like, "We all should eat dinner together! This is the ultimate hang! We're a cult!" But now I understand that people need to take space to keep their heads on straight. So, little factions of the tour kind of splinter off, and you find your meal buddies or you eat alone. Every once in a while, maybe once or twice a tour, there is a big meal, to keep morale high. But doing share plates with eleven people with varying food restrictions also gets a bit complicated, and sometimes you do wish you'd just gone for that miso soup alone. Especially before a big show.

Natalie with oysters.
Photo by Neelam Khan Vela.

When I was younger, I'd never gotten deep on fancy foodie stuff; I couldn't afford it. It was like a mysterious universe behind a curtain. But at a certain point my financial situation changed, and all of a sudden I wasn't always looking for the cheapest thing on the menu. I had expendable cash for the first time and I started to understand the culture of "Okay, I'm traveling and I want to see the best that each city has to offer." After years of seeing food as just a way to survive, I started to see the art in it. When I was younger, I would've been like, "Oh my god, this is so *bougie*," but it's an American myth that a really great meal with a bunch of people and some good wine has to be bougie. So many cultures just do that no matter what; the premium cost of high-quality food is a very American thing. In some places good eating is just a given.

I remember my first time getting tapas in Barcelona. I think it was during Primavera Sound in 2016. I went alone to this spot known for having the best tapas in the world. I did have a band with me, but we must've all decided that day to go on our own weird journeys. I knew about this one lunch counter and I had heard that it was *the* spot. I didn't know any locals at the time, so there was nobody I could ask, "Could you take me here and show me how to read the menu? Or show me how not to over-order?"

If I could speak Spanish, I probably would've been able to eat there alone just fine—people can sit alone at a counter and eat— but I went into it thinking I was gonna have this glorious solo experience, like in the movies where the food critic sits alone at a fancy restaurant and has a transcendent meal. But after I ordered, the guy behind the counter looked at me and laughed a bit; he couldn't speak English but he was trying to insinuate that I should pace myself. Tapas is not meant to be eaten alone.

I wanted the full experience; I wanted all the tastes. Plates just kept coming out—there were pickled things, patatas bravas, smoked seafood, crazy vegetables. It was wild. For the first couple of dishes I ate everything because I come from a background where you clean your plate. But that quickly became an issue. There was this beautiful, majestic raw tuna steak in front of me, and I remember it well because that was the point where I couldn't fit any more food in my mouth. It felt so awful to waste anything, so I was just shoving it in while the waiter grinned at me—as if not wasting it would make me look less like a tourist.

It's funny—as you get more successful, your access to foodie culture blossoms a bit more, but what fades are the automatic personal connections. You might be struggling on tour when it's just two people, but in that case the promoter might want to show you around, be your guide, and give you everything because you have nothing. It's a catch-22. Even when you have less money, you'll probably connect more with the people around you out of necessity. But once you're doing better and you can get the fancy stuff, you may be stuck eating it alone.

Opposite: Natalie backstage at the Greek Theater in LA. Photo by Neelam Khan Vela.

Food as a Love Language, or Not

by Greta Kline (Frankie Cosmos)

Of all the contributors to this book, I've shared the most meals with Greta Kline, my bandmate in Frankie Cosmos for eight years. But a lot of what she writes about here takes place before I joined the band, replacing her then-boyfriend Aaron on drums. Anybody who's listened to Greta's music will know that she's a keen observer of the world around her; the meals that made up her formative tour experiences left many impressions that she's generous to share with us in the piece that follows.

Greta hits on many important themes in her essay, including how food affects romantic (and platonic) relationships between bandmates and how age differences in bands inform attitudes toward food. I've watched her navigate these questions in real time and was even present for the shocking anecdote that concludes this piece. I already miss eating with Greta on the road, but I know we have many more meals ahead of us as friends—and I have a feeling we'll enjoy them even more. *–LP*

I was eighteen when I started touring in bands, but all my bandmates were in their early-to-mid-twenties. I viewed them as adults and duly followed their examples in self-care. Some of my bandmates smoked cigarettes, some showered in the mornings, some brought a pillow on tour, and some never had dinner and spent all their per diems on alcohol. Over the years I formed habits and learned tricks of the trade from my perceived elders, whether they knew it or not.

I realize now that they were only a couple of years older than I was, and that it wasn't such a good idea to emulate a lot of their habits—does swigging whiskey really kill the germs in your throat? Why did I think that? We had a lot of fun, though. I remember my first full-US tour with seven of us (two bands, I was in both). Seven New York residents in sunglasses and skinny jeans, walking into a McDonald's in North Dakota asking for iced black coffees. No cream, no sweetener. The people who worked there were like, "What do you mean?" We felt out of place but in an exhilarating way. On tour I felt I was always walking in front of a green screen, catching glimpses of myself among ever-changing backdrops.

I've always been a sort of picky eater, and at some point in my twenties I started referring to my diet as "tan feed"—like an animal's feed, my slop is just anything beige and bland. It soothes my throat and binds whatever hell is swirling around in my stomach. Cupcakes and bowls of cereal became staples; it got to a point where every meal had to be chased with a sweet carb. My old bandmate David used to say I had a sugar addiction, but I would argue back that I was allowed to have a vice—I didn't drink or smoke like most people in bands, so my masochistic diet was just my hard-earned little treat!

For some of my earliest tours, there were three of us: me, Aaron, and Gabby. Aaron was my boyfriend, but Gabby was more of my partner; each took turns feeling like the third wheel. I sometimes wonder if Gabby felt resentful toward Aaron because she took care of me so much. Gabby and I were constantly getting food together and splitting meals, like a couple would. For breakfast at diners, one of us would get fried eggs and toast, while the other would get cornflake-crusted french toast (we could then do what we called a "split and split"). For late-night gas-station dinners, we would split a block of cheese, a two-pack of peeled hard-boiled eggs, and a bag of salt-and-vinegar chips, and then each get a Lindt chocolate truffle for dessert. It was true connection, our bodies in sync on every level from food to sleep to music.

Aaron often seemed exasperated or annoyed by me and Gabby—our jittery energy, silly games, and constant chatter. Sometimes we would give him some space by slipping away together. I have a few distinct memories of times like that. Sitting in the window at City Feed in Boston, eating sandwiches purchased with our well-loved shared punch card, talking about my relationship. Or sitting in the van when cops raided a house show we were supposed to play in New Orleans, eating handfuls of sunflower seeds for dinner. She was like my babysitter, and we often joked about my feelings of inadequacy as a "band leader" (and my irrational fear that my parents were secretly paying her to be in my band).

We gossiped in the back seat, embroidered, cackled. Sipped single-serving cartons of almond milk to complement the dry cereal in our mouths. Or popped the dry cereal into a mouth full

of almond milk. Whatever worked! I guess what I'm trying to say is that eating, however disgusting, can always be a love language and a bonding experience for people in bands. Gabby helped me learn how to care for myself in a lot of ways. She was more perceptive than I was and helped me work through my toxic romantic relationship as a true close witness. Aaron and I had some good times, but at its core it was just an imbalanced relationship—I viewed him as an older authority figure on how relationships should be, how bands should be, how I should be. Instead of trusting my instincts, I told myself I was wrong a lot of the time.

I felt out of control and a little crazy for a lot of those tours. I think part of it is that I was often hungry and didn't know how to nourish myself. Years later I found myself surrounded by bandmates (particularly Luke) who prioritized mealtimes. It also coincided with being a little more successful and thus having a little more freedom. When we started booking tours to include a day or two off, Luke and Lauren would always try to book an Airbnb with a kitchen and make a delicious meal for everyone. Meanwhile in my DIY touring days, we would mostly stay "healthy" by eating handfuls of spinach straight out of the bag.

While we were never all in the band at the same time, there was one Frankie Cosmos tour in Europe where we had some dates with Aaron's band, and he rode in our van a couple of times. There is one instance we joke about, a food-related difference of opinion that plainly exemplified how incompatible my relationship was. On a cold nighttime drive, we stopped at a gas station and Aaron asked if I wanted anything. I asked him to pick out "some fun chip" for me.

Now, I don't know what you think of when you hear "some fun chip," but to me that means something a little funky—maybe pizza-flavored Pringles, or Cool Ranch Doritos. Because we were in Europe, there were even more enticing options: Monster Munch, Paprika Pringles, even Cool Ranch, which over there is called "Cool American."

He brought me back a bag of plain Baked Lays. We broke up a few months later.

Opposite: Greta with a delicious snack. Photo by Yuki Kikuchi.

PROMOTER SPOTLIGHT:
SHANNON LOGAN

Shannon Logan. Photo by Kevin Morby.

Shannon Logan was a top pro tennis player on the Australian junior tour when chronic illness sidelined her for a couple of years. Just as she started to compete again, she was hit by a car on her bike, sustaining head and neck injuries that would put an end to her tennis career for good. Music became the central character in her life, helping her through this brutal period and shepherding her through to the next chapter.

Before long, Shannon was selling records from a local market stall, and she eventually opened Jet Black Cat Music—a record shop located at the very corner where her bike accident took place in Brisbane's West End. As the shop became more embedded in the local scene, Shannon started promoting shows: In-stores were the natural start, followed by bigger shows, a beloved festival called Nine Lives, and a concert series in cherished rural locales in Queensland and New South Wales.

But Shannon isn't your average promoter. She hosts bands at her home, shows them around Brisbane, introduces them to her mates, and makes them feel like a part of her incredible community for however long they're in town—and beyond.

Frankie Cosmos had the full Jet Black Cat experience in 2017, and I only learned speaking to Shannon for this book that we were the first band she brought over! I couldn't believe it. Her hospitality was so innate and so memorable, it seemed like she'd been having bands stay over for years. Since then, she's hosted many more artists, including more than one contributor to this book. In fact, as I write this, Weyes Blood and—who else?—Kevin Morby are slated for some upcoming Shannon time. They are so, so lucky. *–LP*

Well Fed, Well Caffeinated, Well Swum

as told by Shannon Logan, Jet Black Cat Music Meanjin (Brisbane), Australia

You know what? Most bands are foodies. I mean, food and music go together, right? They're kind of . . . they're like siblings in a way. It's not like, "Aw, it's just 'cause those bands have a bit of money and they can spend another five-to-ten more dollars on a meal than others." Most bands are well into food. It's something that really excites them, and it makes a tour go to a whole new level if that's something that's woven into it.

I toured this band called Glass Beams—who are amazing—and they're all very much into looking after themselves while they're touring. They drink a little bit but not tons, they're excited about food every day, and when you give 'em the rough itinerary on things, they're just ready to roll. And I think it's that thing with musicians: They wanna have a good time, but they wanna have it for a long time, and it's gotta be sustainable. That means looking after yourself by not just supporting the communities that you're moving through and the people within them, but also making sure you're putting good stuff in your body.

We did a four-day tour with them across four different locations, traveling every day, but they were well slept, they were well fed, well caffeinated, well swum—you gotta have swims along the way! And when I dropped them at the airport, they were like, "We've never done four shows in a row, and we should probably be absolutely wiped out right now, but we feel so energized and gig-fit!" It felt like a beautiful holiday, and they got to play some music while doing it.

But like I was saying—we're bringing people from outside our communities into our communities. I feel like it's such a privilege to be able to host, and it's also a real responsibility for us to support the businesses in our communities by taking touring artists around. For example: Sharon Van Etten, I took her to breakfast when she was here in December—and she's just the sweetest person you'll ever meet—and that night at the gig, she was raving about Alphabet Cafe and Avid [Reader] Bookshop. And all of those businesses told me the following weeks that people came in who'd never been there before. They were at a Sharon Van Etten gig, and she was rattlin' on about these amazing places, and it kind of prompted them to go and try something new! And because someone that they really admire was getting behind it, it was like, "We wanna go and check that out." And that is only a tiny bit of that positive ripple effect.

Obviously social media is the thing that everyone's on now, but sometimes I think that it can be used in a really positive way—like a band putting a photo up out in front of a place, or even just a nod to an amazing cappuccino here or whatever; people get around that so hard! And cappuccinos for you, as I've discovered touring a lot of you Americans in particular, are very different to cappuccinos for us! I was on tour with Toro y Moi last year and took them to Alphabet because they make the best cappuccinos, and Chaz [Bear] was like, "What? I have chocolate in my cappuccino!" And I was like, "Yeah, man! That is the reason why it's called a cappuccino; what are you talking about?" It just opens up so much more interaction and conversation. It's just the best!

Opposite: Breakfast at West End Coffee House, next to Jet Black Cat. Lao sausage with wok-fried egg, rice, herb salad, and tomato-chili jam. Photo by Luke Pyenson.

All of these cafés and places, all of them are just so—"Decorate our walls, decorate our counter with all your tour posters, Shan!" Because it feels like it's a win for everyone. People love to interact with the feeling that a touring band is in town; they don't just buy a ticket and then go to a show one night and it's done. It's this feeling like you almost have a little seat in the van, and not in a creepy or fan-y way, just feeling like you're sharing that special thing beyond just the promoter and the artist and selling tickets. It's so much more than that. The community of Brisbane restaurants and cafés is very independent—like Jet Black Cat Music— and there's a real pride in hosting.

I used to be a full-time tennis player. I used to be on tour, you know? I was always on tour, and it ticks many of the same boxes. I went full-time when I was sixteen, so I would be taken in by local families in whatever areas I was traveling in. When you're a kid, you get a bit homesick when you're on the road, but the host families always made me feel very looked after and very much like I became part of their community. It definitely made the biggest difference. As an elite athlete, it allowed for me to not have to worry about certain things and focus on being the best version of myself so that when I did play, I was feeling good and calm and rested and fed.

It takes some intention to be on tour, and to not let those things slip. Because I think that unless that's part of your inner narrative—that food's important and all that—then you just kind of eat whatever's there, and it can often be the first thing to go. And it usually has a knock-on effect as well—if that goes, then your sleep gets a bit bumped, your exercise gets a bit bumped, then you're really struggling to get through tour because you're wiped out. You don't often always have that break in between—it might be back for a day or two and then you're off again. It kind of chips away at the thing that you find the most enjoyable, the reason why you're doing it, if those other things start to go. So it's kind of nice to be able to—in a little way—keep that on track for people. I do get a lot of bands that just say thank you way too much. They're full of so much gratitude, and I'm just like, "Thank you for saying thank you and for being grateful, but like—this is how you *should* be treated, you know?"

I grew up in the country, and my parents have always been very much the people that, it'd be like, "Oh, you've gotta go around to the Logans' for a barbecue!" There were always people staying with us growing up, and Mom and Dad just loved hosting people. I think that old-school hospitality, it's a dying breed of people who still do that and do it well. So I think maybe my nature, and then how I was nurtured, and then that early path on the tennis tour—it's pretty in me; I just can't *not* do that! I couldn't put a tour on and be lazy, like, "Whatever, they'll just eat, they'll just go there, or whatever." I'd just prefer to not do it at all.

Diverticulitis

by Nick Harris (All Dogs)

I first met Nick Harris, a guitarist and former guitar tech, when his pop-punk band All Dogs opened for Frankie Cosmos on tour in 2015. Like many folks I've toured with over the years, he was vegan when we toured together. And I remember him extolling the vegan restaurant scene in Philadelphia, where he lives. It's true; the vegan restaurants there are some of the best in the world!

But Nick's story leaves the territory of dietary restrictions behind and brings us into the tough realities of managing (and not managing) a serious chronic illness on tour. There are myriad reasons why this can be challenging to touring musicians, not least among them our shaky access to good (or any) health insurance. And I think Nick's message has a special resonance in light of pandemic-era conversations around paid sick leave and deferred medical care. Not cheerful stuff, to be sure; we're lucky he has a sense of humor.

At the time of writing, Nick's getting his graduate degree in counseling psychology and no longer tours professionally. His guitar-tech days are over, but All Dogs—long on hiatus—is now "semiactive." It's as healthy a setup as I've heard of, and not surprising for someone as wise as Nick. *-LP*

I love the Descendents. So I was excited when the band I was working for was asked to open for the Descendents back in 2017. But there I was: huddled in a backstage bathroom stall trying to puke as quietly as possible. Sadly, this was a familiar situation at that point in my touring career. It all started almost a decade earlier when I was sitting in an art history course.

Despite liking this class and this college, I dropped out a few months later so I could go on tour for most of the year. I had gotten pretty good at dropping out of college by this point. If I remember correctly, we were discussing the cultural importance of the Vietnam War memorial when I couldn't take it anymore. I calmly informed my professor that I was going to drive myself to the hospital because my stomach felt like it was being repeatedly hit with a sledgehammer.

Two weeks? Three weeks? A month? It's hard to remember how long my stomach had been hurting, but when I was sitting in that classroom, I knew it wasn't going to just go away. I had tried everything that the early-twenties version of myself could think of:

various strains of weed, twenty-five Camel cigarettes daily, Miller High Life, Cap'n Crunch, ignoring it. Surprisingly, none of that worked, so I had to admit defeat and drive myself from my college campus to Abington Memorial Hospital.

The doctor asked for my symptoms: "Sometimes it's the worst pain I've ever felt," "Sometimes it feels like I just got off the Gravitron," "I'll throw up and it doesn't feel any better," "Sometimes I'll have a fever," "I smoked a joint of OG Kush mixed with Strawberry Haze, and my stomach still hurts."

Diverticulitis.

Pretty much the entire hospital staff said that I was the youngest person they'd ever seen diagnosed with diverticulitis. The instructions they gave me would become a common refrain I'd hear from medical professionals over the next several years of my life: "Here's a prescription for antibiotics. No solid food for a few days."

I went back to my house in South Philadelphia and took it easy for a couple of days, and then suddenly my pain was gone. A few weeks later, I was in another hospital: "Here's a prescription for antibiotics. No solid food for a few days." This cycle repeated until finally the instructions changed. "Nicholas, this is clearly getting worse. I think it's time we discuss surgery." The recovery time for the surgery was six weeks.

"That simply wouldn't work," I informed my doctor. "I can't take six weeks off! My band is about to go on tour with Smoking Popes, and we're getting paid a hundred dollars per night." I couldn't understand why he thought I was joking.

Before I knew it, I was in a van driving halfway across the country to start that tour, with my stomach screaming at me. This would be the routine: stomach hurts, go on tour, smoke a bunch of weed or drink a bunch of whiskey to dull the pain, go home, see a doctor, ignore their advice, go back on tour. The doctors (and the internet) told me all types of different things: Don't eat nuts, don't eat seeds, eat nuts, eat seeds, drink a gallon of water a day, don't eat black pepper, avoid fiber, eat fiber, get surgery, stop ignoring this.

Some relief came when a holistic doctor in California put me on an intensely restrictive diet for twelve weeks. After I finished the diet, a year passed without an episode of intense pain. Then another year. Then another year. I was in the clear. Then it started again. I missed a couple of shows on a tour with the Offspring when I went to an ER in Michigan. Once again a doctor asked me if I'd consider surgery. Then my jaw dropped when he said I needed

Nick backstage in 2015. Photo by Luke Pyenson.

to be eating a diet that consisted of meat and pretty much nothing else. That simply wouldn't work, I informed the doctor: "I can't do that! I'm vegan, and I have a flight booked for tomorrow to meet back up with a monthlong tour." I couldn't understand why he thought I was joking.

I conceded a bit; when I met back up with the tour, I ate grilled chicken at catering, and over the next few weeks, I felt better. I was in the clear. Long gone was the chain-smoking vegan; now in my late twenties, I was smoke-free and eating steaks, and my stomach felt great. But later that year, there I was, doing everything in my power to prevent any of the Descendents from hearing me puke my guts out. I might be slightly off chronologically, but it gets tough to keep it straight because of how many times the same thing happened. Writing all of this reminds me of the old cliché, something about repeating the same actions and expecting different results is the definition of insanity. But when your rent, insurance, and groceries depend on going on tour, you go on tour.

I went on my first tour when I was a teenager and it became all I wanted to do with my life. By the time I was touring for a living, the thought of doing anything else seemed ridiculous. If I wasn't willing to miss a tour that paid an entire band a hundred dollars per night, I certainly wasn't going to get surgery and miss a tour that would pay my rent for the next few months. But then there I was in 2019, at the Austin airport, grabbing my suitcase from baggage claim and experiencing the absolute worst pain I have ever felt. It was day one of a six-week tour where I was working as a guitar tech, and I instantly knew that this was a bad scenario. I made it less than a week before I was in an ER in New Mexico.

I was having a familiar conversation with a doctor ("You need to go home and take care of this immediately"), but I informed the doctor, "That won't work. I just started a six-week tour. I need to finish this tour." This time the doctor didn't think I was joking. This time the doctor told me it was time to go home, and maybe it was the pain, but I listened. I apologized to the band, I flew back home that night, and within a month I had surgery scheduled.

They removed the broken part of my stomach, and I haven't had anything even resembling a symptom of diverticulitis since. Writing this has sparked all sorts of internal questions: Can nonstop touring be done in a healthy way? What is the relationship between beneficial nutrition and constant travel? Is perpetually being on the road worth the "real-world" sacrifices? More than anything, I want to leave you with this: If anyone from the Descendents happens to read this, I'm really sorry if you heard me throwing up.

Eating Right

as told by Dawn Richard

It's uncommon if not unheard of to transition from the trenches of mainstream pop to the world of indie. But this was the path taken by the artist Dawn Richard, formerly a member of the pop groups Danity Kane and Diddy - Dirty Money before striking out on her own in 2011. Now signed to storied indie label Merge Records, Dawn is making waves in the indie world with her singular approach to electronic music, enlightened collaborations, and electric live shows. She is also the proprietor of Papa Ted's, a vegan food truck and events producer, in her native New Orleans.

Dawn's frankness and honesty about food and body image on tour will ring true for a lot of people, including those whose work puts them in the public eye. She also reminds us that performing is a physical act that requires proper fuel—if you've been lucky enough to see Dawn live or even watch her music videos, you'll understand why this is especially true for her. We could've talked to Dawn for hours and hours, but we're lucky to have this condensed and edited piece born from what was a very memorable conversation. *-LP*

Eating on tour wasn't healthy in Danity Kane—oh my god, the junk-food level! And I think all artists do that; we eat the worst we could ever eat. Hideous food. And because our shows run from ten to eleven p.m., we're not eating a full meal till midnight or one a.m., so we eat horribly. We gain weight or we lose way too much weight, and then we sleep in a tight spot. It's wild! In Danity Kane, we had nobody to help us live healthy on tour, but if you got fat, they gave you a call.

At the beginning, nobody knew who we were, so we would get a meat-and-cheese tray, and then water. That would be the extent. We would put stuff on our rider and then nobody would give it to us. It was all restaurants and fast food, but I was dying for something that felt a little bit more soulful—I'm from the South, so I like homemade food better.

Then when I got with Diddy - Dirty Money, I walked backstage and it was like a fucking kingdom. It was so glamorous, but it was like window-shopping. At first, I was like, "This is amazing!" And then I thought, "None of this is for me, because none of this is anything I would eat!" And every time we'd go to a show, none of the things we liked were there—we just feasted on whatever was brought for *him*, and we had access to that.

In Diddy - Dirty Money, it was even more extravagant because we were with Puff's money, so we ate *wealthy*. We ate beautifully. He had a chef, so we ate what the chef cooked, and that was beautiful. Puff didn't have to worry about, for example, if he started gaining weight or he wanted us to lose weight because, "Oh, you're too skinny, you're too fat . . ." He would just tell his chef, and we would have protein shakes made. Or his chef would put him on a diet, and he'd have grilled chicken instead of fried chicken.

He was kind and we ate well. It's not like it was horrible, but there is the boss and then there is you. We were group members, but he was also the boss. If you came out of shape and you looked crazy, the conversation would be had, and he'd send whoever he needed to send to make sure you were at the level you needed to be at. But there was no conversation of, "Okay, guys, we're gonna make it a point that you're healthy and that we're eating three meals a day . . ." No.

The sad part is—the amount of money we spend on marketing the *visual* of what an artist "should" look like, but we don't care about how they attain it. It's about how quickly we can make you thin or pretty or, for men, bulky and muscular, without giving you the regimen to figure it out. And that's something that I had to figure out on my own. What keeps me healthy, I learned, "Oh, it's running." Not taking a shake and starving yourself for six days. I learned, you know, you can eat three meals a day and then run, and then decide what works for you to be able to sustain your *talent*.

I've been vegan for six and a half, almost seven years. My dad got diagnosed with lymphoma, and that's the reason I became vegan. He and I did veganism together, and I just loved what it did for me so much that I stuck with it, and he and my mom did too. We created a life based off of it because of his health, and now it's all I know. So it was imperative for me to be consistent with it while I toured, because it meant something more than just eating well. It meant staying consistent with my father—it was something bigger for me.

It wasn't until I was touring on my own that I realized I even had the ability to ask for anything. But I would rather have the venue put more energy on their lighting tech, for example, than worrying about having a vegan option for me in the green room. It gives them more energy, so when I get to the venue and I'm like, "Do you have a haze machine?," they're like, "Let me see what I can get!" because they're not wasting time trying to find me kale chips.

Budget is a huge thing when you're funding it yourself, and you have to get very creative. But when you're broke and you're doing things DIY, sometimes your health is the last thing you're thinking about. You're just trying to get your show up and you don't realize by the end of the night you're dead, you have nothing left. I had to realize how important my health is. I have to dance—people forget that it ain't just singing. It's two hours of full choreography with vocals, so stamina is important. It's essential that I be healthy and be able to eat healthy.

So I started learning how to cook. When I'd tour overseas, I'd book places that had kitchens so that I could cook for myself, and I also learned to route the tours to places that catered more to my dietary requirements. In places like the UK or Switzerland, I'm always able to find organic stores, and they have really cool mom-and-pop delis. I can get basic things like organic produce and organic crackers, and a lot of times I'll get fresh fruit juices.

But I do have cravings for certain things—and of course, sometimes I miss Creole food. So I travel with a bottle of Zatarain's hot sauce! I would die if I couldn't eat well.

Eating in the Van

by Brian "Geologist" Weitz (Animal Collective)

The first time I saw Brian "Geologist" Weitz, he was onstage wearing a headlamp and gesticulating wildly over a mosaic of synthesizers, gadgets, and children's noisemakers. It was the spring of 2005, and I had just graduated from high school. Brian's relatively obscure, weirdo art band, Animal Collective, was beginning to make a name for themselves; they'd already hooked me the summer before when I first heard their album *Sung Tongs*.

Less than five years later, Animal Collective released *Merriweather Post Pavilion*, which catapulted them to international recognition. They got about as big as an indie-rock band can get, but even through the haze of their experimental music and their anointed positions as the unwitting kings of indie rock, they remained relatable to me. I could tell that at their core, they shared something fundamental with Real Estate. Deep down we were all just geeky friends from the suburbs piling into a van and chasing our musical dreams.

So it's no surprise to me that the story Brian has chosen to tell for this collection concerns Animal Collective's early days. It's as awkward as it is exciting for a young band to start "growing up" and taking itself more seriously. In this case, Brian has to weigh the newfound benefits of getting to the show on time against his better instincts to keep junk food (and its odor) out of his body, his tour van, and, as it turns out, his memories. *-AB*

Around 2006, when leisure time decreased and rest stops increased, I decided that I hated eating in the van. We cared more about soundchecks, so hitting a mid-afternoon load-in time became crucial, and if we didn't want to wake up super early, the drive had to be as compressed as possible. But there were opposing forces slowing us down. We had a couple of crew members and often let the opening band ride with us. More unsynced bladders meant more stops. We also had more gear and merch than could fit in the back of one van, so we had two trying to keep pace with each other, and when one van stopped, the other did too.

With all those stops, when mealtimes came, we had to ask ourselves the question, "Are we eating it here or getting it to go?"

Breakfast was an issue—some people were annoyed to wake up early and rush to get on the highway, only to get off a few exits later for an egg and cheese. By lunch we had our eyes on the clock and the speedometer, doing miles-per-hour math in our heads to see if we would be late. I always hoped we'd opt for eating at rest stops as quickly as possible before leaving, but if we were behind schedule, I could hear the phantom monitor feedback in my brain, warning of how the night might go if we didn't make up time by eating in the van. Even when the stop wasn't around a meal, someone always got a bag of chips or a drink. Regardless of the situation, food and food packaging were always in the van.

I didn't actually mind the smell while eating, or even right afterward. The moment of disgust came upon reentry after being out of the van for a while—the particular way the lingering smell hit me when I got back in. That smell was waiting for me after load-out, but the next morning was when it was the worst. Over the weeks, it snowballed into a combined odor of fries, Doritos seasoning, whatever weird chemicals make Subway smell like it does, and slowly dissolving wax from the paper cup that someone left a couple of inches of melting ice in overnight.

The smell zapped any feeling of refreshment, even if there had been time for a decent night's sleep and a shower the night before; the whole cycle started over again regardless. I'd immediately feel heaviness from the air in the van. Breakfast didn't help, and then people would worry they were getting sick, so we'd dissolve Emergen-C tablets in plastic water bottles and drink those fairly quickly. That just made us have to pee more, so we stopped at gas stations and got more food to add to the atmosphere. And it wasn't just in the air; eventually you could see and feel it. The knobs and display panel on the stereo were coated with potato-chip grease, and the light would reflect off of them in a haze, like a parking-lot oil stain.

My aversion to eating in the car remains to this day, though if you see my car, you'll realize I don't really care much about cleanliness. Especially since I've had kids, it's pretty disgusting, and food is a big part of the problem. But finding months-old Cheerios, peanuts, or raisins crushed into the seats doesn't bother me; they're different from the snacks we had in the van in those early AC days and don't bring to mind the smell of yesteryear's fast food.

It's a different story on family road trips when fast food and gas-station snacks come into the equation. I'll always push for us to avoid the drive-through and eat inside. If someone wants a bag of chips, I'll go for it, but I won't be happy, and if it's a rest area with tables and grassy space, I'll suggest we just eat there. Even if I pass on the food myself, the smell gives me psychosomatic rider gut (AC slang for how you feel after eating too much rider food). I'll feel like I ate too many gummy worms and regret the plastic bottle of soda I didn't even drink.

Now as I write this, it is early 2021 and we're still mostly isolated due to Covid. About a month ago, one of my children had a doctor's appointment, and across the street from the office is a McDonald's. We have a deal that if they have to get a flu shot or any other needles during their checkup, we'll go to McDonald's afterward for french fries. Because of Covid, eating them there wasn't an option, so we got the fries to go and, not wanting them to get soggy or cold, we enjoyed them in the car on the way home. I even opened a pack of sweet-and-sour sauce and balanced it in the spare-change holder.

The next time I got into the car, I was greeted by the familiar smell of french fries—still lingering, as it does—and I almost couldn't bring myself to leave. When I did, I went inside and texted my bandmates to say how much I missed them. We haven't played together in sixteen months now. We've canceled tours and studio sessions, and it's still unknown if we'll be able to do any of those things together for another year yet still.

I'd give anything to be on tour again, getting into a van every morning with that smell, forcing down that artificial orange Emergen-C flavoring, and everything else that comes with it. Instead of making me sick, it just makes me miss my friends.

The Brownie Incident

by Eric Slick (Dr. Dog)

Eric Slick might not be a household name, but he should be. Perhaps best known as the drummer for indie-rock mainstays Dr. Dog, Eric is an extraordinarily talented multi-instrumentalist who plays with a lot of people in the indie-rock universe. A few years ago, he and I really bonded at an airport. Real Estate had played right before Dr. Dog at a festival in Indianapolis, and Eric and I had some time to kill during a layover. Fittingly, I can't remember exactly when this was or where we were. Sometimes the fog of touring life blurs things together like a hazy dream. I do, however, remember the conversation Eric and I had.

Like me, Eric has struggled with weight and compulsive eating throughout his life. In some anonymous airport terminal somewhere, surrounded by unhealthy temptations, Eric and I got to talking about this, and how we related to food and body image while playing in indie bands. I knew I wanted Eric to write about these concepts for this book, but I had no idea he'd relay a story so heartfelt and hilarious that we'd name an entire chapter after it. *-AB*

In 2006, I was on my first real tour with a Frank Zappa tribute act called Project/Object. We were different from the other Zappa bands because we had the real alumni onstage with us, namely Ike Willis, Napoleon Murphy Brock, Ed Mann, and Don Preston. I was eighteen years old and naively struggling my way through turn-on-a-dime time-signature changes, a massive set list, and wild extended improvisations. On the good nights, I was listening to everyone and playing the music with the utmost respect. On the bad nights, I was completely lost in the abyss, facing furrowed brows and death stares from my childhood heroes. To say I was an anxious mess is an understatement.

My relationship with food has always been terrible. When I was young, I was rewarded with pints—nay, *gallons*—of Breyers ice cream anytime I achieved some menial task or even just as a prize for eating my two overloaded plates of dinner. This is not to slight my parents; I'm just saying I learned to stuff my emotions down with food at an early age. Their love language is gift-giving and food. You can ask my therapist.

Girls wouldn't talk to me. In fact, people wouldn't really talk to me or take me seriously. So my teenage years were spent trying to knock the 50 pounds of overweight fat off of my body. I tried everything I could.

In the summer before my junior year of high school, I began to starve myself every once in a while. It worked. The starving and growth spurts helped me get down to 150 pounds. My family was worried, but I shrugged them off. I finally had friends—lots of cool, new friends who suddenly liked me because I was thin. It's a dynamic that I've resented my entire life.

Fast-forward to May 10, 2006, in Rochester, New York. We were at a venue called Milestones, an unremarkable bar with miserable bar food. I was on my first tour and had no clue how to eat or treat my body with any modicum of self-care. My per diem was somewhere around ten dollars, so I'd load up on Rockstar Energy drinks and boxes of Honey Bunches of Oats that I would eat by the fistful in the van. Dry, milkless, disgusting fistfuls of cereal. I was probably destroying my metabolism. I had gotten down to some painfully thin weight on that tour. I learned about binge eating and found plates of cubed cheddar cheese that I demolished when no one was looking.

When I arrived backstage that night, I noticed a huge plate of unwrapped brownies. We weren't a huge band, so I had never heard of riders, let alone any kind of healthy backstage grub. Since I was alone, I stuffed four of them in my mouth. I didn't even think about it. I ate them in a fog of low blood sugar and teenage angst and went onstage to soundcheck. Project/Object soundchecks could be brutal. We were running through some particularly difficult material, and I was probably getting chastised for rushing a measure or playing something wrong. I felt dejected. When I stepped offstage, it felt like the entire ground collapsed underneath me.

"FYI, everyone," our keyboardist shouted, "those brownies backstage are special!"

My heart sank. I veered my eyes toward him in what felt like slow motion.

"What do you mean?" I asked.

"Oh no, how many did you have?"

"I had four."

The owner of the club burst through the raggedy twin doors and looked directly at me. He was a wonderfully flamboyant man, with an aura and look that reminded me of John Waters. He smiled and exclaimed:

"Oh, *honey*. Somebody get this poor boy a quesadilla!"

Everyone in the room began to laugh, and I felt the fluorescent lights turn to pitch black.

My bandmates pulled me aside while they could and described to me what pot brownies were and what my night was going to be like. I think they felt sorry for me, but there wasn't much they could do. They scooted off to a vintage guitar store while I vomited in the open stalls of the Milestones bathroom. I did end up having a quesadilla on the outside deck, to get some fresh air. It dawned on me that I was going to have to play a three-hour Zappa show while fully under the influence. We would do two sets that were an hour and a half each with an intermission. This was going to be the longest night of my life.

The show began. As usual, we had about forty nerds in the crowd. Some were tapers; some were just Zappa fanatics who couldn't believe they were seeing their favorite songs get played for the first time. I was in my own personal nightmare hellscape. Our bassist, Dave, was humping his StingRay guitar in my direction during the first song, "The Little House I Used to Live In," and I thought he was an animated clay demon. I kept telling myself, "It's all muscle memory. You know these songs. You can power through it." It was getting worse. I was dehydrated and unbuttoning every button on my soaked striped shirt.

I somehow got through the first set. I went backstage to decompress for a minute, but when I got back there, something insane happened. There was a full camera crew. Bright lights. You have to understand how DIY this tour was. We didn't get a ton of press, let alone a full camera crew. Everyone had neglected to tell me that a local cable access show was going to cover us that night.

Of course, this was not your average cable-access show. I was confronted by a man in a rabbit costume holding a smaller rabbit puppet with a tiny puppet microphone. His name was Pisspot. Let that sink in. He gestured toward me and shoved some dollar-store fake rabbit teeth into my mouth. The camera light went red. "Just play it cool," I told myself. "It's a rabbit."

Pisspot spoke in a high and irritating cartoon voice. "HI, ERIC! How are you? I heard you had some SPECIAL BROWNIES. Can you tell us how you're *feeling*?!"

I looked at Pisspot with disdain. I was confused. I didn't want anyone to know about what had happened. What if I had friends who could eventually find this? I looked Pisspot in his beady little puppet eyes and felt a deep pang of hatred.

I threw the rabbit teeth down on the vomit-splattered backstage floor. I got through the rest of the show, albeit barely enough to call it a good one. It took several days for the brownies to wear off.

In the coming years of touring, I would struggle with my weight and vacillate between the bi-poles of obesity and low body mass index. It wasn't until two years ago that I learned that this was a form of disordered eating. In a way, the pandemic has been a blessing. I'm working with a registered dietitian and I'm finally getting things under control. I've learned a lot of lessons about eating the hard way.

And Pisspot, if you're reading, I forgive you.

Baba

by Steve Sladkowski (PUP)

Guitarist Steve Sladkowski of the Toronto rock band PUP will forever hold a special place among the contributors to this book: He was the first person to send us an essay. And when I read it, I got a little—in the words of fellow Torontonian Mike Myers—verklempt.

Steve and I have some mutual friends, but another thing we share is eastern European heritage, and touring Europe brought us both closer to our ancestral homelands than ever before. Frankie Cosmos only got as far east as Hungary and Poland, and even then only one show in each. But bands like PUP who play heavier music tend to have bigger audiences in that neck of the woods, and they're more likely to hit more central and eastern European cities on tour. It's in this part of the world that Steve's story takes place.

In putting together this collection, Alex and I were careful that the pieces we included wouldn't perpetuate the stereotype that musicians drink heavily while on the road. But in Steve's relatable and vulnerable essay, he homes in on the truth that, oftentimes, heavy drinking goes hand in hand with heavy eating. And when the two dovetail with sudden loss, everything becomes even more difficult to manage. *-LP*

One of the most mundane aspects of European touring is the transportation: Mercedes Sprinters outfitted, in varying degrees of fanciness, to make a grumpy band's life slightly more comfortable. More often than not, a Blu-ray player and several charging ports help you pass the hours crisscrossing the continent while you struggle to remember what language you need to butcher when ordering a coffee and pastry or a plate of beige protein, root vegetables, and a beer. PUP was on one such tour, in one such Sprinter, in early 2018 when I found out my grandmother had died.

The night Baba died, we were in Budapest for the first time and were shocked to find out how many people from eastern Europe loved the band. After the gig, my bandmates and I were standing idly by the merch table and speaking to people who had traveled from Poland, Russia, Ukraine, and Belarus for the show at Dürer Kert because it was, at that point, the closest we had ever been to any of those places.

A few excited young Belarusians came racing up to me, begging to do an interview. They had read somewhere that my bandmates Nestor and Zack were Ukrainian Canadian and that I was Belarusian Canadian and wanted to ask questions about our families and touring experiences for a Belarusian-language zine and radio show. As the interview finished, the guys from Minsk and I spoke in the green room and tried to determine, in stilted English, where my grandparents were from—it was unclear then and it's still unclear now—and as the clock struck midnight, we came to the conclusion that it would have to be somewhere around the city of Navahrudak and drunkenly marveled at how small the world can be. I found out the next morning that my grandmother passed right around midnight central European time.

As the van rolled out of Budapest, I was overcome with memories of my baba that centered around food and eating: how she would hand-crimp her homemade pierogi with the tines of a fork; my dad, aunt, and grandparents, crowded around the kitchen table at my childhood home in Toronto, eating headcheese doused in vinegar (my cousins and I were nauseated by the smell); the year or so when Baba seemed to confuse different tomato sauces and served after-school snacks of pizza with a Tostitos base or tortilla chips with Ragú for dipping. In the backyard of that Toronto home, her vegetable garden bore bumper crops of tomatoes, cucumbers, sorrel, and herbs that were used for soups and pickling, or just picked off the vine and eaten over the sink in the middle of an August heat wave. I wept silently as I realized it was logistically and financially impossible to get back for the funeral. "Don't worry too much," my dad consoled me when we finally spoke on the phone. "Baba would have been horrified that you'd skip a gig for her."

When we returned to Europe again at the end of 2018, though I didn't know it at the time, I was struggling with depression for the first time in my life. I avoided this recognition through drinking booze and placing a premium on heavy traditional central and eastern European comfort food meals with my bandmates, with our crew, or by myself: Erika's Eck in Hamburg for schnitzel and sauerkraut and beer; goulash and dumplings and beer when back in Budapest; beer and pickled onions and beer and meat that looked suspiciously like headcheese in Prague. But all of these meals were placeholders, a gastronomic undercard for the main event: when my bandmates and I arrived for our first-ever Polish show.

For PUP's three Slavs, Warsaw was the closest any of us had ever been to our grandparents' homelands. By the estimation of Google Maps, I was some 400 kilometers (248 miles) from Navahrudak. Our tour manager, Dan, was well aware of how stoked

Opposite: Pierogi. Photo by Steve Sladkowski.

we were and made sure to find an Airbnb in the heart of Warsaw. We white-knuckled the eight hours of driving from Berlin, through torrential downpours, on two-lane highways pockmarked with potholes, to ensure we could have a night and half a day exploring and eating our way through Warsaw before the gig. The crew and band were still feeling residual vection as we dropped our bags in the bedrooms of a Soviet-era brutalist apartment. The rain was still falling as we wandered into a corner store in search of vodka and pickles to properly toast our first time in Poland. I found myself seamlessly ordering vodka in some strange Polish-Belarusian-English hybrid that caught the shop clerk's attention: "You have no accent!" she exclaimed with surprise in a similarly stilted English as the young punks from Minsk; I told her about my grandmother.

Meandering back to the apartment, we found ourselves shoulder to shoulder around a table in the tiny kitchen and quickly polished off a bottle's worth of vodka shots chased by pickle spears. This gave us the energy and buzz we needed to search out a traditional Polish restaurant, so we set back off into the rainy evening in search of more food and drink. Steaming cups of borscht and platters of pierogi and sauerkraut and rye bread and more booze were brought out as we ate and drank and tried to figure out how to pronounce złoty. All the while, there was a static in the back of my mind, some sort of psychic feedback that I couldn't quite figure out. "Ignore it," I told myself. "Just drink more and it'll go away."

My attempt to put on a happy face stayed with me throughout the rest of our time at the restaurant. We ended up back at the kitchen table in the apartment eating weird peanut-flavored corn snacks chased with selections from the mixed bag of beers that are collected, rolling around, in the back of the van on every European tour. I quickly passed my ten-drink nightly average for that tour in an attempt to ignore that static that had further settled over me.

It worked until I was alone in the bedroom trying to crash. Lying down to try to force sleep that wouldn't come, I realized we were traveling in the same Sprinter we had been in when I'd found out my grandmother had died: the same charging ports and Blu-ray and well-worn blue upholstered bucket seats that made your ass go numb on any drive longer than five hours. Something inside me cracked and provided a moment of clarity. Perhaps it was being so close to my paternal grandparents' birthplace, or perhaps it was the unlikely odds of experiencing two life-changing events in the same foreign vehicle, but whatever it was, I knew I couldn't keep drinking the way I had been; I knew I needed help to deal with whatever was driving the impulse.

I was up until five a.m. searching the Ontario Psychological Association website for a psychologist in Toronto. By the time I woke up, still drunk and unsure if I had dreamed much of what happened in that bedroom the previous night, I had received an email back from a psychologist and a potential booking for the first week back from tour. I replied immediately and took the meeting. He is the same therapist I see to this day.

дзякуй, бабуля. я сумую па табе.

Dinner in Poland. Photo by Steve Sladkowski.

Chapter Three

Always Eat with Your Pack: Exploring Family and Identity on Tour

There's always the potential to miss an important family holiday on tour, and one of the most significant I can recall was Thanksgiving 2009. It remains the only time I've spent that holiday away from home, but in a lot of ways, it was an exciting era for me and Real Estate—we had just released our first album to rave reviews, and we were in the middle of our first cross-country tour.

Still, missing the yearly traditions I'd grown so fond of with the people I loved most weighed on me heavily. This alienating feeling—the feeling of *missing something*—while out on tour is all too common, especially as it relates to family and friends who are left behind. What I didn't know then was that my young band had already begun forming into a kind of family unit of its own.

In vans traversing every highway all over the world, roving nuclear communities are singing along to obscure power-pop songs; sharing their life stories, dreams, and regrets; or sitting awkwardly in all-consuming, deafening silence. They're stopping for fast food or at Whole Foods, and making hurried forays into gas stations for snacks—some reach for beef jerky, some popcorn, others a banana. Everyone knows who's getting what before they've even parked.

For better or for worse, touring band dynamics can closely mirror family dynamics. And just like my family at home, my band family has basked in inexplicable highs and weathered devastating lows. We have formulated our own language indecipherable to "outsiders" and generated extraordinary, formative memories together. We've mourned difficult losses and opened painful interpersonal rifts with one another that might never heal. I love my bandmates dearly, but just like with my parents and my siblings, my feelings for them are nuanced and complicated.

Within this complex web of social dynamics, strong personalities can—and do—emerge. When you're constantly associated with one small group of people, it can feel essential to carve out your own identity in order to foster some sense of individuality. Growing up in my at-home family, I did this with my musical tastes. On tour, I do this with food. Someone has to be "the one who always knows where to go for dinner"—why shouldn't it be me?

This process, often illogical and fraught with conflicting emotions, is both a product of and a contributing element to the band-family dynamic. But sometimes, it's bigger than all of that. With the opportunity to travel so widely and so frequently comes the chance to consider how you might fit in—not just into your band but into the world around you.

In this chapter, we'll hear from the Uruguayan artist Juan Wauters on discovering his national cuisine—kind of—in unexpected stops on tour; we'll get the scoop on what Stephanie Phillips of UK punks Big Joanie calls the "diaspora dinner run"; and we'll learn how dogsled mushing informs the eating habits of Alaskan John Gourley of Portugal. The Man. We'll also cover veganism—of course—with the help of ex-vegan Robin Pecknold of Fleet Foxes and current vegan icon Sadie Dupuis of Speedy Ortiz. It seemed healthy to include both viewpoints.

All of that, plus a pickle-and-sauerkraut-filled recollection of the love story underpinning Sylvan Esso, a pho-fueled fight instigated by travel editor and ex-rocker Sebastian Modak, and more.

The following pieces remind us that the band-as-chosen-family touring unit intrinsically reflects the behaviors and dynamics in one's own personal history. And that wider explorations of the world through touring can both broaden and narrow our focus, bringing sharper images of personal identity into view. *-AB*

My Savior, My Destroyer, the Subway Veggie Patty

by Robin Pecknold (Fleet Foxes)

Growing up in the carnivorous, cookie-cutter suburbs of New Jersey, I did not encounter many vegetarians, and I can recall meeting absolutely zero vegans. It wasn't until I moved away to a progressive college in Vermont and started booking my own DIY tours on Myspace that The Vegan became a ubiquitous figure in my life. It was also around this time that I started listening, with reverence, to Robin Pecknold's band, Fleet Foxes.

Robin isn't a vegan anymore, but he was back then, and his essay that follows looks back with a sober and critical eye on how he aligned much of his identity (on and off the road) with his aversion to animal products. Just as the choice to "become a punk" or "be a hippie" can signify far more than musical tastes, veganism for many isn't just a simple dietary choice—it's a lifestyle. *-AB*

I chose the wrong decade to be vegan. In 2001, at age fifteen, fighting postpubescent bloat and newly (though superficially) enamored by suburban punk zine ideologies, I vowed to consume no animal products, to wear no leather, to be a friend to The Animals, yada yada. I felt like Saint Augustine of Hippo after his conversion by Ambrose of Milan. "I am vegan," I announced, Lisa Simpson–like, to crickets at the dinner table. "I am vegan now. I require specific treatment in all ways."

The small thrill I felt as my mother got up from the table to prepare me special meals should have been my first clue that this vegan conversion was more a plea for attention than a well-reasoned stand against animal cruelty. But the die was cast, and so was set in motion the next sorry decade of my gustatory life.

At first, committing to veganism in Seattle meant building an exciting and unique new mental map of the city. Hundreds of restaurants and stores became instantly invisible to me, while a small handful became essential. A new cadre of friends and role models materialized. I was raised in an atheist household, so it was ironic (yet fitting) that, aside from a few patchouli-soaked relics, the only restaurants I could regularly eat at were faith-based establishments catering to Buddhists, Ethiopian Orthodox Christians, or Jains—believers who regularly or entirely eschew animal products on religious grounds.

Fitting also because my veganism did in fact feel religious, providing all the sanctimony, elitism, deprivation, and stricture of the faiths that my father had railed against at the dinner table. But also the sense of belonging, morality, community, and empathy—not to mention a bevy of useful falsehoods. All important psychological needs I'd somewhat missed out on in my rational, secular youth.

My commitment to the principled, deprived life of The Vegan dovetailed precisely with my commitment to the principled, deprived life of The Musician. By the time I was twenty-two, I was on tour, playing hundreds of shows worldwide in my band, Fleet Foxes. I repeat, this was the wrong decade to be vegan. The mainstays I turned to in Seattle were nowhere to be found on the wide-open road. There may be essays in this book about some plant-based revelation a bass player had at a New Nordic temple in Stockholm, or a shockingly convincing medium-rare vegan burger at a hip street market in Madrid, but there were next to none of these joys to partake in back in 2008.

In 2008, our options were Clif Bars, Twizzlers, Spicy Sweet Chili Doritos (no casein!), that weird Loving Hut restaurant chain owned by a problematic cult leader, and plain pasta with olive oil. Maybe bagels with Tofutti "cream cheese" on a good day. Pickings were disgustingly slim. Daily protein requirements and nutrient macros were yet-undiscovered concepts. At the same time, that raft of gray-area questions that required satisfactory answers at home—"Do they cook the fries in vegetable oil? Are there egg whites in this? Do they butter the crust? Do they use the same grill for the meat and the black-bean burgers?"—fell by the wayside on week seven of a van tour in the middle of nowhere, Mississippi.

Touring in 2008 was malevolent and hostile to vegans, no question. But I had already loudly announced my veganism. It was My Thing. I had Othered myself from the world, from the group, from the tour. And one can't just renounce their faith at a random truck stop once they're sick of eating chocolate-chip Clif Bars and being hangry all the time.

I was left with one small oasis in this hellish desert. The skinflint Van-Tour Nationwide Culinary Map at the time included the

The Subway Veggie Patty.
Photo by Luke Pyenson.

following restaurants: Waffle House, Pizza Hut, McDonald's, and, very occasionally, if we had sold enough T-shirts the night before, Cracker Barrel. It also included Subway.

My savior and my destroyer became the Subway "Veggie Patty," a gray-brown mélange of unidentifiable vegetal ingredients, damp from the microwave. Mouthfeel of sieved paper pulp or marinated sponge. Flavor nonexistent to net negative; it was so powerfully antiflavor that it siphoned and destroyed the flavor of anything surrounding it. Just a volume of calories, a shape, a wet wallet of mashed peas and binding agent around which I'd pile lettuce, spinach, carrots, salt and pepper, and oil and vinegar, all encased in a sleeve of dubious bread.

This sandwich was my go-to, most every day, for months. My sad friend, the Veggie Patty. We had a codependent relationship in which we validated and amplified each other's deep flaws and misconceptions. Each afternoon, I'd emerge from a new gas-station Subway with a fresh Veggie Patty footlong serving as my self-flagellation bludgeon and cross to bear. I'd intuit subliminal eye rolls from the rest of the band, each gnawing on Slim Jims or (for all I knew) drinking fortifying meat slurry. Between soundcheck and showtime, they would deadlift guitar amps while I counted the malnutrition spots on my fingernails.

I imagine one reason this book exists is to illuminate just how important food can be to keeping the vibe going on tour. Seeking out new restaurants or novel regional dishes can be the best part of a touring day, especially conducive to bonding and blowing off steam after hours spent hauling gear, driving, or performing in similarly mundane spaces day after day. An eye for food can turn touring into a great communal scavenger hunt when otherwise it can be an exhausting, repetitive slog. I spent years missing out on this release early in our touring career, and it's my main regret from back then. It was mostly just me and my floppy Veggie Patty sandwich, like a couple of antisocial tweakers in the sleeping loft, freebasing sanctimony.

Once my five years of relentless early-twenties touring came to an end in 2012, I gave up on veganism. I reasoned that eleven years was enough, and that I had done my time in the Animal Suffering Reduction penal colony. These days, the vegan landscape has changed dramatically since the beginning of my career. I'm on tour now with many vegans who seem to be getting by just fine nutritionally and who report back on the mind-blowing restaurants they find in even the smallest cities.

Despite my comfortable omnivorous lifestyle, the Veggie Patty—whether from nostalgia, or something more sinister—occasionally still beckons. I had it again recently for the first time in years. It was gross as ever, but this time I knew something I didn't back then: It wasn't even vegan.

Confessions of a Vegan Reply Guy

by Sadie Dupuis (Speedy Ortiz; Sad13)

For another take on veganism, we turn to one of indie rock's sharpest writers and best-known vegans, Sadie Dupuis of Speedy Ortiz and Sad13. Friends from my hometown played in both Sadie's older band, Quilty, and Speedy Ortiz, but a penchant for forming bands with folks from Newton, Massachusetts, is only one of her many qualities. At the Krill-Speedy double bills that saturated the Boston area's DIY venues between 2011 and 2014, I remember being blown away by Sadie's musicianship, songwriting, and soaring lyrical wizardry. It was no surprise at all that they were the first band to "break out" of our scene.

Now a published poet with two celebrated books, a record-label boss with an imprint under Carpark, a musicians' advocate, and, yes, still a hardworking road dog (now with book tours too!), Sadie offers words that resonate far beyond the scenes that fostered her early projects. Including, as I'm contractually obligated to mention, in the album bio for Real Estate's 2020 masterpiece, *The Main Thing*. But if you really want to see Sadie's handiwork, check out the comments section of your favorite vegan restaurant's Instagram.

She explains below. *–LP*

Have you come across the portmanteau "rockognized"? It's a cutesy stand-in for when a rock musician gets—you guessed it—recognized in public. The year 2006 claims the first and only entry on Urban Dictionary: "Totally rockognized Fred Durst at the McDonald's in Hollywood." You get the gist. Rockognition can be a surreally flattering experience, especially when your level of rock fame is somewhere between micro- and Polly Pocket–sized . . . like mine. It is most impressive when your non-rocking friend or relative happens to be with you, thus validating your woefully undercompensated career in their eyes, or maybe just in your eyes through theirs.

Here are some places I was wowed enough by getting rockognized that I made a joke about it online:

- On a tour of a haunted prison
- Getting my teeth cleaned
- Floating down a river in an inner tube
- Guitar Center (But they only knew my even-less-popular band, so it *was* cool.)
- While parallel parking (TWICE)
- In bookstores (I call this getting "poetry rockognized." It should probably just be "recognized," but it's not as funny without the pun.)

One way (the only way?) that I cannot relate to Limp Bizkit is that rockognition would never happen to me in a McDonald's. I've been vegan for eighteen years, so if I enter a McD's, it is to use the bathroom without buying anything while praying no one gets weirdly mad at me about that. No, not even the fries are vegan— I am so sorry to disappoint you. If I visit Ronald's house, it's a stealthy in and out, way too brief a visit to get spotted.

The rockognizing rules I just made up state that it can't happen at a rock show; the rockognizer's gotta discover you outside the context of rock. I have woefully few hobbies or interests besides music, but veganism is one of those hobbies-interests-lifestyles-deathstyle determinators. So a pretty big pie slice of my rockonnaissances have happened at plant-based restaurants, one of the few types of places I leave the house for.

The other week, I was waiting for a coffee in Philly (okay, I leave the house for caffeine too) when I experienced a newly gratifying form of rockognition adjacency. "You're Sadie, right?" asked a fellow line queuer. I didn't know him, so I expected I'd hear a sensible follow-up question, like "From Speedy Ortiz?" But then he surprised me with a theretofore unheard sentence: "I recognize you because you always leave comments on vegan restaurants' Instagrams." And it's true; I've become a somewhat prolific vegan reply guy. I was proud that this other Philadelphian had taken notice.

For the past decade-plus of constant touring, I've used my itinerant road dogging as a thinly veiled excuse to hit up a roster of vegan-friendly spots around the world. If we're playing in Portland, Oregon? It's time for a classic barbecue platter courtesy of Homegrown Smoker. Pittsburgh gig? I will risk my wheat allergy, pop a Benadryl, and go hard on decadent pierogi from Apteka. I'm not gonna pretend like I didn't move to Philly in part for its legendary vegan scene, which has only gotten better; big shouts to Pietramala (tonnarelli!), Primary Plant Based (fiddlehead fajitas!), and the Tasty (chilaquiles!) for enduring my boatload of IG enthusiasms.

I love my local and faraway haunts with equal fervor. So when the pandemic took my bands off the road for a few years, it did not stop me from excessively chiming in on long-distance restaurants' posts, dropping a lot of repetitively worded demands for them to freeze and mail me a brunch special. Here are some recent comments I've used to deface the food pics gracing the grid of Columbus, Ohio's Two Dollar Radio Headquarters:

@twodollarradiohq: SUPER HOT blackened carrot taco special

@sad13 (that's me): looks mailable

@twodollarradiohq: *posts a bulgogi mushroom bibimbap*

@sad13: i feel one could just slip that little egg into an envelope and send it to philly with only a stamp or 2 for postage

@twodollarradiohq: do you like your Soy Beef Tacos classic style or Bulgogi seasoned?

@sad13: i dunno, which one is easier to mail?

Austin, Texas's Bouldin Creek Cafe has long suffered my overzealous fandom. I became its neighbor in 2008 during my stint as a college dropout/video-store clerk/bartender/burger-joint FOH/freelancer/punk no-goodnik (deep breath), and it was there I found the best vegan breakfasts I've ever encountered. After I moved back to New York, I remember ringing up Bouldin Creek to leave a semi-inebriated voicemail, begging for their indisputably perfect tofu-scramble recipe. They never called me back, for some reason . . . ? I did learn how to dupe their chipotle pecan pesto, and every time I whip it up for a potluck, I swear I am the evening's most temporarily adored person. If only they'd FedEx over some zucchini migas, I'd happily eat whatever surcharge Bouldin deemed fitting. Before eating, duh, the migas.

In 2018 Speedy Ortiz collaborated with a handful of restaurants across the US and the UK, including the aforementioned Bouldin Creek. They'd name a menu special after something Speedy-related, then donate proceeds to a local food-justice org. We called it the "You Ate the Title" Tour, a riff on our song "You Hate the Title"; it was a crafty excuse to go to all our beloved spots and fan out in person. (All-caps nota bene: TIP 30 PERCENT OR MORE

IF ANY OF YOUR FOOD GETS COMPED BECAUSE YOU GOT
ROCKOGNIZED!)

Speedy has toured with some of my all-time favorite bands, and
I've been featured on songs by laughably out-of-my-league artists.
I tell you this not to brag, but to insinuate that I am capable of
playing it semicool when faced with celebrity. Yet nothing makes
me quake in my fan-filled boots quite like getting a follow-back
or a DM from a plant-based pizza truck (hello there, Lil'l Nonna's).
So in planning that food tour, and in plotting some edible merch
a few years later, I found myself typing to restaurateurs with
disproportionate exclamation points, so much so that you'd think I
was corresponding with Jennifer Lopez. But can't we all agree that
Lagusta Yearwood is the JLo of vegan chocolatiering?

Music, as much as I love and need it, doesn't give me the
intoxicating feeling that a beautiful meal can. I'm not completely
shabby with a chef's knife, but I can't take a bite of risotto and
rattle off every top note. Enough years in and around recording
studios have given my ears a good sense of how different sounds
are crafted, and I've learned how to replicate the ones that excite
me. Which is fun and rewarding, but it comes at the cost of some
right-brained wonder. Music brings me fun and joy but not much
mystery. For mystery, I turn to food. And for escapism amid the
weirdness of touring, I turn to food too.

I grew up with my mom, an artist and teacher whose creative
talents extended to cooking, and my few culinary tricks are solely
thanks to her patience. When we moved out of New York and up
to rural Connecticut, her closest neighbors were dairy farmers,
who also raised calves for veal—a by-product of their industry.
Seeing the penned-up baby cows who lived a short walk from us, I
had a "Lisa the Vegetarian"–style moment of truth. I cut animals out
of my diet for good, and not too long after, I went vegan. But there
really weren't plant-based options in our neck of the literal woods.
A local paper actually ran a story about how our school cafeteria
had started making hummus, since one kid couldn't eat anything
on the "normal" menu (thank you, cafeteria workers).

When I visited my dad, he was more into dining out. Growing
up, I'd spent weekends with him popping into whatever Greek
diner, hot-dog stand, or dollar-slice spot he was loving that month.
Once I became vegan, there were still tons of veggie-friendly
options for us to explore, like the long-running Caravan of Dreams
and Angelica Kitchen. On the three-ish-hour commutes to and
from New York, which I now theorize groomed me to be a traveling
musician, my dad and I would scheme over where to grab a bite
next. Food reportage was a way to connect from afar, and when I
started touring, I'd keep him posted on where I'd eaten. He passed

in 2015, but when I find a really exceptional dish, I still catch myself thinking that my dad would love it.

My fellow touring musicians were the first other vegans I knew, so seeking out and hyping up hot spots is a kind of secret handshake passed between us. Regardless of whether a van benchmate eats vegan, we still share delight in trying new places, supporting the good ones year after year, and getting any amount of legitimate nutrients in our diets. There were so few tasty places to eat vegan for so long; you do not want to know what vegan cheese tasted like in the dark ages of the mid-2000s. As the diet's benefits for individual and environmental health have become more widely understood, it's been mind-blowing to find restaurants around the country innovating with technically astounding plant-based foods—like Crossroads Kitchen's artichoke oysters on the half shell, holy moly!

So yeah, when I'm excited about a new vegan-y thing, I like to share that excitement . . . maybe a little too much. This is how I wound up having to go private after receiving, among other forms of ridicule, Twitter death threats for posting a picture of a May Wah vegan lobster. (It had a cute smiling face! Leave me alone! You would've posted it too!) And that zealotry compels me to comment excessively on vegan restaurants' socials—even though it's clear none of them are gonna mail me those brunches.

If the two to nine of you out there who know my music encounter me in or out of a vegan restaurant someday, please say hi. I promise I'll be thrilled to meet you. But if you recognize me for vegan posting? That'll be the real chef's kiss, the rockognition that lets me know all my one-sided love letters to tofu tacos have been worth it. And if you're down to freeze something vegan and drop it by a post office for me? You know I won't stop you.

...But I Found Blackberries

by Alex Bleeker

In all my years of traveling I've met a number of colorful characters, but none of them have impacted me as deeply as my old bandmate Alex (yes, we have the same name). I knew the guy before we wound up playing music together, but on tour we developed a close bond—a brotherhood. He's a one-of-a-kind weirdo—a true freak with a unique and gentle soul, but just like my real brothers, he can really get under my skin. All the same, I'm grateful to have been able to reflect on one of my favorite memories and the time we spent "playing in the band" together. *-AB*

The Iceman was actually a very warm and friendly guy. I'm not exactly sure how he got his nickname, but like so much of the vocabulary developed on tour, it just kind of stuck. It might have been because he was a stone-cold lead guitar player. Or maybe it was because he was a hippie spiritual type and nicknaming him after a fabled New Jersey hit man made some kind of demented, incongruous sense. Whatever the reason, he was my bandmate and my best friend, and he had a penchant for getting lost.

I once "lost" The Iceman (Ice, for short) for two whole hours between soundcheck and showtime. When he finally turned up, just in time to play the gig, he told the rest of us that he'd taken a historical trolley to the other end of the city and wound up in an architectural museum. When he'd noticed it was getting dark, he'd figured that it was time to wander back to the rock venue. Another time, standing in the pedestrian main drag of Charlottesville, Virginia, we lost him again. Then the rest of my bandmates and I noticed an elderly character skipping along and playing a pan flute—following diligently behind him and capturing the whole scene on video was The Iceman.

Of course, "lost" is only a relative state of being, and from his perspective, Ice was always exactly where he was supposed to be. In so many ways, a curious and adventurous individual like The Iceman is well suited to the touring life. Sure, he was on the road to play music every night and he was good at it, but I get the sense now, looking back, that these road trips were also like pilgrimages for him. He was there to experience all that was there to be experienced, and to see what there was to see, however obscure. Most touring musicians I know possess this kind of wanderlust to some degree, and it can be a valuable asset on tour—one that leads to all kinds of fun and memorable situations. Sometimes, though, it can be a real pain in the ass.

There's a kind of rosy projection that's often associated with a rock-and-roll tour, this sense that we're always singing "Tiny Dancer" together in the back of a tour bus somewhere. Don't get me wrong—truly special moments happen on tour, and I'm grateful for them, but they can be few and far between. The untold truth is that more often than not, touring is dominated by static monotony and logistics. The bulk of what your favorite musicians are doing out there on the road (measured strictly in minutes and hours) is simply getting from place to place.

By 2013, when this story took place, I had a split-identity touring style. Real Estate had found our stride as a reasonably successful mid-tier indie band. Our tours were booked by an agent and structured by a team. Out on the road we were usually accompanied by a tour manager, a person who handles all the day-to-day logistics that come with playing shows every day for a few weeks. It's a stupid joke, but we'd sometimes refer to our tour manager (or TM) as the "paid bad guy," meaning that it was their job to deliver the bad news (usually relating to daily wake-up times).

In between Real Estate tours, I'd head out on the road with The Iceman and the rest of my much scrappier band, the Freaks. The Freaks were far less successful financially speaking, which meant that we booked our own shows, we crashed on people's floors every night, and we did *not* have a tour manager. This kind of touring is often referred to as DIY—do-it-yourself. It's a lot of fun but can also present challenging intra-band dynamics, chief among them being, "If we are doing this all ourselves, who is the paid bad guy?"

The Freaks were a great group of musicians who were not motivated by money or fame, but by something much more important: fun. Playing music in a different city every night is intrinsically fun, but at every level it still requires a fair amount of mind-numbing logistics. The Iceman in particular did not take well to this harsh reality. He was on tour for the cultural and musical *experience*, and making it to the next city on time for a leisurely soundcheck was not primary among his concerns. He liked to sleep in, and he did not like to be rushed.

The Iceman. Photo by Alex Bleeker.

Of course, to a large degree he and I were on tour together for the very same reasons, but I was the chief songwriter in the Freaks. I'd done a lot of work setting up the shows, and I felt a nagging sense of responsibility to honor all our commitments with a professional demeanor. One particular night we played a blistering set, after hours, at a high-end restaurant in Athens, Georgia. I remember a foreboding sense of trepidation and many confused faces as we wheeled our heavy amplifiers past scores of unsuspecting dinner guests. Nevertheless, after service ended, a small team of us cleared away all the tables and chairs and an entirely different kind of crowd showed up to hear us play.

Night after night, a good show on a DIY tour is everyone's collective goal, but it can be rare. The Freaks were on fire that night, and The Iceman played particularly well. Afterward, we ambled back to a friend's living room to bask in the glory of a job well done. We stayed up too late, we had a few beers, we laughed a lot, and then we got into a fight.

I don't remember where we had to be the next day, but I do remember that we had to drive for roughly seven hours to get there. Touring musicians are conditioned to withstand an ungodly amount of time in a van, but any drive over six hours can start to feel excessive. Having assumed the de facto role of "unpaid bad guy" on this trip, I sternly suggested that we wake up at seven-thirty a.m. sharp so that we might be on the road by eight. The Iceman, as you might imagine, was not enthused by this prospect. We had an awkward argument about time management and respect in front of our gracious hosts, and then we took a vote.

In a nonhierarchical, flat-structure organization such as a DIY band on tour without a manager, majority rules. Somehow The Iceman had managed to garner overwhelming support for his point of view, and we agreed to sleep in until ten, soundcheck be damned.

Needless to say, by eleven, I was behind the wheel of our big red Dodge van feeling pretty stressed. We were going to be late and there was nothing we could do about it. A loaded silence tends to settle into the tour van on days like this. I'm sure that I made a few passive-aggressive comments at some point, but midway through the drive a collective sense of urgency had been firmly established. We had long abandoned the dream of a soundcheck and were freshly united in the pursuit of our new goal: to get to the show in time to play at all.

Somebody had to pee. I pulled off the highway and into the parking lot of an anonymous gas station. Like a pit crew during the Indy 500, we all nodded to one another and filed out of the van with tactical precision. "Let's make this quick." Moments later, bladders emptied and Swedish Fish in hand, we were all back in the van. All of us except The Iceman.

Where the hell was he? He was lost again; he'd completely disappeared. Over the years we'd grown to appreciate this quirky personality trait of his, but this really wasn't the time. Something cracked, and the van broke into open frustration.

"Where the hell is he? Somebody go and check the bathroom."

"He's not there."

"He's not in the gas station at all; he's gone." He's just gone.

Ten long and excruciating minutes later, he emerged seemingly out of thin air and casually opened the door to the van. I was seething. I had been sitting in the driver's seat utterly embodying the role of the *unpaid* bad guy, anxiously rehearsing what I might say in my mind. Eventually I just let him have it.

"Dude, I need you to take this more seriously. We are late, you can't just wander off like this, we are all waiting for you, we need to get to the show on time, and this is completely DISRESPECTFUL AND UNACCEPTABLE BEHAVIOR!"

The Iceman looked back at me with heartbreaking earnestness. His eyes were wide, his mouth open just a little bit, and he had something in his hands. He stretched his palms outward and said to me with pleading innocence,

". . . But I found blackberries."

PROMOTER SPOTLIGHT: CHANTAL MASSON

Chantal Masson has promoted shows in her native Dijon, France, with the group known as Sabotage for the past decade. She previously worked as an administrator at the Université de Bourgogne during the day and threw shows at night, but she is now happily retired (from the former). One of the brightest and most unique in the constellation of legendary DIY promoters across Europe, Chantal is known for hosting (and feeding) bands with her partner, JP, at their lovely flat in the center of town.

My first stay with Chantal was the result of a rare booking error— we showed up in Dijon the night before we were actually meant to play, but Chantal insisted on hosting us all the same. We participated in an indie rite of passage—making pins on her pin machine as we snacked away on generous helpings of local food and listened to vinyl. In the middle of a tiring monthlong tour, I can't underscore enough how much better this was than playing a show.

I still have the pin I made that night, which simply and proudly displays the words *ÉPOISSES LIFESTYLE*. Gourmands know this means she served us the delectable triple-crème cheese her region is known for. The pin is safely stored with my most treasured tour ephemera, and though I'm not lucky enough to eat époisses very often, I always think of that night when I do. *–LP*

Les Soirées chez Chantal et JP

by Chantal Masson, Sabotage

Dijon, France
Translated from the original French by Luke Pyenson

I have volunteered, for the past decade or so, with a group called Sabotage that puts on indie concerts in Dijon. My role is to welcome, host, and nourish visiting artists, and I love it! My partner and I are lucky to have a studio and courtyard on the ground level of our apartment building, and over 250 groups have spent at least a night there.

I welcome bands the same way I would my friends—simply and, I hope, warmly. The band could be coming from the US, the UK, New Zealand, or Germany, but we're sure to quickly uncover many things in common (in particular, taste in music!). We often weave strong connections, and years later I'll receive texts saying, "Hey, do you remember me? We have a day off between Paris and Lyon. Can we crash at your place for the night?"

"Of course, guys, you're welcome!"

In my opinion, food and lodging are important for bands. Tours are long and tiring, and eating frozen pizza or kebabs with fries . . . it's all right for a day or two, but after two weeks you've had enough. I prepare simple things, usually pasta with pesto and sun-dried tomatoes, artichokes, and parmesan; cheese from the market; and, of course, bread and wine—that's inescapable in France! On summer mornings, we can have breakfast on the balcony; croissants taste even better in the sunshine.

I pay attention to everybody's individual tastes—vegetarians, folks with allergies . . . But I've seen "vegetarians" throw themselves at jambon and saucisson. "Beware, it's meat!" I say, and they respond, "I know, but we're in France; it's not the same!"

Some of my guests have created surprising combinations, like spreading époisses (one of our prized local cheeses) on a croissant. But why shouldn't they? And one particularly starving musician—I won't say who—after drinking a pretty good amount of red wine as we picnicked, ate sushi wrapped in pizza. He slept well after that!

Yet another, returning to my place after having played at a very posh venue, brought a bottle of wine the promoters gave him. Which was a grand cru that must have been worth at least two hundred euros. "The right bottle with the right people," he said. So sweet.

Food has a reassuring quality, especially for those traveling from city to city each day. It's the same for lodging. My studio is small, but it's a space with a history, not anonymous like a hotel room. I've stuck photos of all the bands who've passed through on the walls, and each time a new band stays, the reaction is the same: "That's my next-door neighbor!" or "We toured together!" or "I played with that band"—one big indie-music family. In that way, my guests feel like they're staying with old friends, which is important to me.

Nights often finish around a bottle of wine (or, honestly, a few bottles of wine) or some beers, talking about music and politics, listening to records (usually "oldies" from the '80s)—it's the same type of night we'd have with our local friends. No borders for music lovers.

In the courtyard at home in Dijon. Photo by Chantal Masson.

Ella's Deli

as told by Amelia Meath (Sylvan Esso)

Seeing Sylvan Esso play live has always been a transcendent experience for me. Sure, their music is great and they're excellent performers and all that, but watching them, I'm generally feeling something more personal. Amelia Meath and I were great friends in college, and we shared many formative experiences, both musical and otherwise. I was in the room when her early folk trio, Mountain Man, decided on their band name, and their early performances around campfires in Vermont consistently brought me to tears.

When I first met Nick Sanborn, Real Estate and Sylvan Esso were both in Salt Lake City on tour. Amelia told me we were going to have lunch with this guy she'd started a new electronic project with, and I remember feeling the raw creative excitement and energy coursing between them during that meal. Two years later, I found myself standing on the side of the stage at Treasure Island Festival watching them absolutely thrill a crowd of five thousand people. They'd fully realized the potential of their creative bond—of course they had. *-AB*

The first time I met Nick, the other half of Sylvan Esso, I was on tour in Milwaukee and his band Made of Oak was opening up for my band Mountain Man. We kept in touch a little bit after that and were sort of tangentially connected on Twitter, but we didn't really know each other very well. He stopped touring for a bit and was hanging out in his hometown of Middleton, Wisconsin.

At this point I was twenty-two years old and Mountain Man had been hired to sing backup on the road with Feist. I can't imagine being a thirty-three-year-old woman and hiring a few twenty-two-year-olds to be your backup singers—it sounds crazy—but Leslie did this and was so kind to me. It was 2012, and I was about eight months into a year-and-a-half-long tour. I was floating on air because the difference between the dirt-dog touring I was used to and being on a bus was pretty wild. All of a sudden I'd become a twenty-two-year-old fancy lady and I'm on a tour bus and making a day rate for the first time in my life. It was insane. Like, when you hand a twenty-two-year-old three hundred dollars a day—fuck, it was so cool. I was energized, but I was singing backup, which is a totally different vibe.

Nick knew the Feist tour was coming to Madison, right near his hometown, and he wanted to bring his mom to the show. So he got in touch with me, and I got him some tickets and told him I'd have lunch with him. He was just some guy I knew on the internet. We'd yet to have the true friendship moment where I was like, "Oh, I like this person; I really want them to stick around in my life." It kind of felt like one of those bad obligatory tour hangs that you have to do. Often it really seems like a good idea to hang out with a new friend or someone you don't know or your cousin's best friend on the day of a show, but when the time comes it ends up feeling more like a chore than anything else.

So he comes to pick me up, and I'm feeling this way, and also I'm really hungover. I just sort of roll out of the tour bus and get into his car and I say, "Will you just take me somewhere that I can get a really good grilled cheese? That's all I want." And Nick, without skipping a beat, was like, "I know the place."

He took me to Ella's, which was the most surreal and wild Jewish deli in the middle of Wisconsin and was fully packed with all of these hand-painted animatronics that the owner had built. They truly had the best grilled cheese! They also had really good matzo ball soup and my favorite "stunt" order that I still think about to this day: a beautiful and tall pale-green glass of sauerkraut juice with two pieces of bone-dry rye toast for forty-six cents. I wound up going back there specifically to order this a few times. I'm not really sure what you're supposed to do, but every time, I'd eat both pieces of toast and usually dip them in the juice. I thought the whole thing was a joke, but the sauerkraut juice would come out in this custom glass, which itself had this gorgeous tiny handle, and it sat in the divot of this custom green-glass plate for the toast. It was heaven.

Nick ordered a Reuben with matzo ball soup. Honestly, it wasn't really that adventurous of him, but at the time I remember thinking, "This is cool; he's obviously been here before and knows that the Reuben is good." But yeah—it was a total Wisconsinite order. Weirdly, his mom worked there when she was in high school, so it has always been a special place for him and his family.

It was at that lunch that we decided to start a band together. It's a classic thing when creative people get together and start talking to one another. Eventually somebody says something like, "We should collaborate," and usually nothing ever comes of it. But the coolest part about this instance was that I could tell that we were both equally committed to actually doing it. It must have been because we were the members in our respective bands that wanted to take things further. We had never played music together before,

Amelia and Nick backstage at the Greek Theatre in Berkeley. Photo by Leanne Kriz.

but we were once a part of a three-band bill together where the band members made up more than 50 percent of the audience, so I knew where he was coming from. I could see what he was doing and how much he just fucking loved making music, which is rare.

So here we are many years later in Sylvan Esso together, and oh yeah—we're married too. It was a sign of excellent judgment and risk-taking, bringing me to Ella's, because you can't take just anybody to that vibey of a place, particularly when they're grumpy and hungover. In that moment at that lunch, I was like, "Who's this indie guy?" He was wearing a red cardigan and was very nice, but the coolest thing was that I had made this awesome new friend who took me to this wild-ass deli and he actually wanted to make songs with me. That was so exciting.

I keep talking to people about Ella's, and I have to tell them that it's closed now. Oddly, it's become a kind of specific grief process that I've helped a bunch of other people through. It had become a "touring spot" for a bunch of musicians, and talking with a few people about the restaurant, I started to realize that by the time they closed, the food had been bad for like five years. There's a part of you that wants to hold on to it, but nostalgia is a toxic impulse. On that level, it's not a major heartbreak, like, "Oh no, I'm never going to have that sandwich again." But I do miss that sauerkraut glass.

Diaspora Dinner Run

by Stephanie Phillips (Big Joanie)

It's a sign of the times that I first heard Stephanie Phillips's sharp cultural commentary at a Zoom book launch for a mutual friend, but I was already a fan of her music—Stephanie is singer/guitarist of the UK-based Black feminist punk band Big Joanie. She is also an arts and culture journalist. Her nonfiction debut, *Why Solange Matters*, garnered critical acclaim upon its release in 2021, and her articles appear in publications across the UK and beyond.

   Here, Stephanie lets us into Big Joanie's culinary MO on tour—a way of eating steeped in meaning for all three members, who share Caribbean and Black diaspora heritages. Because of their colonial histories and the ingenuity of their people, these are food cultures that tell a story of the entire world in all their layered complexity. Touring can always be an opportunity to learn and connect—sometimes even to see one's own mirror image reflected or refracted through the lens of a new culture. The smartest bands are the ones who understand this and take advantage. *—LP*

It's one a.m. in San Francisco, and my eyelids are starting to drift downward of their own accord. My band Big Joanie, a few friends, and I have made our way to the exquisitely decorated home of a Black woman of Barbadian heritage named Sarah who invited us round after a raucous show at Rickshaw Stop. Sitting in Sarah's living room, slumped on the low, voluminous couch surrounded by Black-centric artwork, books, and records, I feel the familiar urge to doze off unless someone or something snaps me out of it.

    Suddenly, a warm plate of freshly fried plantains lands in my lap courtesy of our host—who instinctively knows that I need sustenance if I'm going to stay awake. I take my fork and dig into the biggest piece. Bringing the glistening, golden-brown plantain to my lips, I cautiously blow on it, cooling the bite-size portion to an edible temperature as quickly as possible. I take a bite, and instantly the crisp, salty outer layer gives way to the soft, sweet, fleshy interior in one euphoric mouthful. My parents often made fried plantains as a snack for me and my brother—it's a familiar flavor I've craved regularly since childhood.

Just like that, I'm back in the room. Eyes wide open, no longer nodding off at the party. I'm ready to be part of the night. Sarah's decked-out speaker system has been blaring old-school R & B, soul, and funk. She turns to me and says, "You're the selector now; what do you want to hear?" I put on Freda Payne's heartbreaking pop hit "Band of Gold" and let her piercing vocals soundtrack the rest of my blissful late-night snack.

That plantain-filled night stands out as just one of the countless highlights that have punctuated our numerous years on the road. I've been playing in bands since I got involved with the DIY punk scene in 2011 and have been touring consistently ever since. With Big Joanie, I've been able to tour across the UK, Ireland, Europe, and most recently America.

I know—we're lucky to do what we do and bring our songs to life every night among friends and fans, but life on the road is far from glamorous. You're away from home, your loved ones, and your bed, and sometimes the most you see of a city is the backstage of the venue or traffic on the way there. Finding some home comforts when you're in an unfamiliar place can help keep you grounded and willing to keep the show on the road.

The Big Joanie tour crew is always majority people of color, with heritages across the Caribbean, West Africa, and Mauritius. For this reason, when we look for comfort, we seek out foods from our home countries, as well as cuisines that connect us to our heritages. The other, more practical reason for this is that we're a large group with various intolerances and allergies—it's easier to choose meals that we know will meet everyone's needs and keep us feeling good during the show.

On show nights, we prioritize efficiency; on rare evenings off— if we have enough energy to venture out of the hotel—we scour the city in search of next-level food finds. The first time we went to Amsterdam, in 2018, we were on tour with Parquet Courts. It was a disaster: Our van broke down twice on the motorway leaving London, and we had to spend all night looking for a rental car. By the time we finally managed to get one, it was too late to start driving, so we set off on the seven-hour drive to Amsterdam the next morning in a tiny car crammed with gear. We barely managed to make that night's show, but feeling invincible after persisting through such an ordeal, we actually played one of the best sets of the tour. It was one of those experiences that brought us together as a band.

Things only kept improving the next day. For lunch, we decided to check out the city's Surinamese cuisine, and it didn't take us long to find Warung Spang Makandra. There was a palpable energy inside the modest restaurant, as if everyone there was meeting a friend they hadn't seen in years. Tables were densely packed together, and we slid into one by the cash register, inches away from another group.

The menu brought together so many regions I didn't realize were connected. Suriname is a small South American nation on the continent's northern coast, but the enduring legacy of Dutch colonialism lingers in its fascinating food culture. Influences from India, Indonesia, West Africa, and elsewhere form the backbone of a cuisine that hums with a personality all its own. I decided to try a sweet pink coconut drink called dawet, whose roots can be traced to Indonesia. It was syrupy and refreshing, unlike anything I've ever had before.

Then came banana fritters followed by roti with chicken curry. The flavors carried enough traces of the Caribbean to be comforting, but they still had a sense of the unfamiliar: the perfect mixture. It was a great start to our Surinamese food journey, which has evolved into one of our favorite tour traditions: Each time we play in Amsterdam, we get a new dish from a new Surinamese restaurant.

We made another one of our best food discoveries back in 2019, while trying to escape our run-down, prisonlike Paris hotel. On the outskirts of the city center, where the Seine meets billowing industrial factories and the bustling ring road, we chanced upon an incredible Antillean restaurant with five or so tables. I wish I could remember the name, but it sadly looks like the restaurant closed down. I do remember the meal.

Not content to try just one thing, we ordered a selection of dishes from across the menu. Before long, the table was filled with hearty portions of grilled chicken, rice and peas, fried fish, plantains, and fish cakes. My grilled chicken leg took up half the plate, and the fish, with its head still on, looked like it had lived a good and bountiful life before it ended up in front of us. Needless to say, it was all delicious. The chicken had a smoky flavor to it, reminiscent of Jamaican jerk cooked the right way—in the oil-drum barbecue barrels known as jerk pans. The fish tasted like it could have been made by my grandma on a special occasion, and that's high praise.

My raging sweet tooth knows no bounds, so it's no surprise my favorite part of the meal was dessert: a dish called tourment d'amour, which translates to "love's torment" and comes from the French-occupied Les Saintes Islands near Guadeloupe. Legend has it that fishermen's wives used to make these coconut-filled pastry tartlets topped with sponge cake when their husbands came back from sea. From the first bite, I knew I would eat this every day if I could. We left that night feeling full, not only from the meal but from simply being in the presence of our own people.

Leaning into the flavors of our ancestors has allowed us to explore more of the world than we've physically traveled to. We've been treated like family at Malaysian restaurants in Manchester by aunties determined to make sure we ate as much as physically possible, and we've made friends in hour-long festival queues waiting for Jamaican food.

And because colonialism took so many people from their original homes and brought them to the Caribbean, South America, Africa, South Asia, and beyond, we've tasted firsthand that geographically distant cuisines often have quite a lot in common. The distinction between Indian and Guyanese cuisine, for example, or Ghanaian and Jamaican, really isn't as widely different as you might think just looking at a map.

Seeing a nation through its food is one thing, but seeing a nation through the food of the people it has colonized is eye-opening. Each mouthful reveals how disparate groups of people were forced together, lived through unimaginable horrors, and still managed to keep the traditions of their home cultures alive, even blending them together to make something new. It reminds me that solidarity between marginalized people is a necessary act if we want to bring down the colonizer nations that tore us from our homelands.

As I write this, I'm about to go back on tour, which means I'll also be going back to the diaspora dinner run. We don't always find somewhere that fits the bill every night; there have been a few times when pizza has had to suffice. But when that special place comes into view, we know it's going to be a good night. Powered by plantains and rice—and everything they represent—we'll always be ready to play another show.

Opposite: Surinamese curry with roti in Amsterdam. Photo by Luke Pyenson.

Always Eat with Your Pack

as told by John Gourley (Portugal. The Man)

I have to admit that I was a bit trepidatious before sitting down to interview Portugal. The Man for this book. Founded in Alaska in the early 2000s and now based in Portland, Oregon, they are perhaps the most well-known and mainstream act included in this collection. So when Luke and I heard through the grapevine that they were "into food" and willing to chat with us, we didn't really know what to expect. Could it be possible to achieve such universal success and still have relatable food experiences on tour? Did these guys ever sweat it out in a crappy tour van, or did they just shoot straight to the top of the Billboard charts?

There's a lot of camaraderie that exists between touring bands, but sadly there's a lot of competition and jealousy that can exist too, especially from less popular acts who feel they "deserve" more success than their contemporaries. Viewed through this toxic lens of "indie credibility," was Portugal. The Man even cool, man?

When we finally got frontman John Gourley on the phone, we quickly realized how ridiculous it was to be asking these questions at all. Not only are Portugal. The Man generous, humble, and, yes, cool—they have definitely paid their dues. *-AB*

Basically, growing up in Alaska, you kind of eat whatever's in front of you. That's just how it goes. There are no restaurants, so it's not like you go out looking for a good meal. You go, "I want a burger tonight," and whatever you want that night, you just go and get what you need to make that food. And it's your energy for tomorrow.

But the quality of the food in Alaska is just so high—I didn't even eat salmon growing up, but as kids we would go catch salmon for our parents' friends. We lived off the Kenai River, so we had these little tributaries where the salmon would get kind of stuck during spawning. We would walk in, pluck out massive king salmon, and just carry them out of the river. It's the freshest food you could find! We ate everything—we ate bear, moose, elk, caribou. Everybody has a freezer full of halibut. Growing up, that was, like, our everyday food. So I think that gave us all an appreciation for food, because the local ingredients were just so good. But we never really thought much of it.

When you first start out touring, if anyone asks another band where to go eat, like, "Hey, where should we go in town to get a burrito?," it's always like, "Oh, this spot down the street gives you a burrito *this fuckin' big* for five dollars!" It's about whatever's the *biggest* meal you can buy. Not necessarily the best. I always thought that was hilarious. 'Cause that's not always what you want to eat before a show!

When we started, we ate for a dollar a day, the whole band. We would get a dollar bag of vegetables, and we had this 5-pound bag of rice. We couldn't even afford a new rice cooker when we started out; they were like fifteen or twenty bucks at the time, and we just didn't have the money. It took days of going to different Goodwills till we found one for eight bucks. But we would just take this 5-pound bag of rice, and in between dates, we'd get a bag of vegetables and throw it in with the rice, and that's all we ate.

I also remember scrounging around in Flint, Michigan, for Whoppers. It was two Whoppers for ninety-nine cents, and we didn't have enough money for everyone to get one. So we were digging in gutters to get three dollars so all six of us could just have a Whopper. That was like 2004, maybe 2005. We put out our first record in 2006, and then we did three dollars a day.

We had actually sold out shows before we realized you got paid to play. We're Alaskans; we had no clue! We did not know what a "guarantee" was. The second time we sold out Chain Reaction [a beloved all-ages venue in Anaheim, California], they gave us pizzas at the end of the show. And we were like, "Oh my fucking god, they gave us pizza! I can't believe it!" And then the next time we came through and sold it out, they gave us like five grand or whatever it was, and we're like, "You get paid to play shows? Last time we got pizza, and we were stoked on pizza!"

Eventually the foodie movement started to spread around the country, and we saw it in Portland, Oregon, where we'd settled. Zach [Carothers], our bass player, worked at a really great restaurant, Epicure, so he was around really nice food and wine. And it was a well-paying job that would let him come and go. Jason [Sechrist], our drummer, worked at the Woodsman Tavern shucking oysters. Our keyboardist, Kyle [O'Quin], worked at Canlis in Seattle. So we would start hitting these places, and that's where the elevated tastes started coming into the band.

I remember Jason saying how much he hated making seafood towers, like, "It fucking sucks, these rich motherfuckers come in, and they order the seafood tower, and I've gotta deal with crab

legs, oysters, all this shit!" We thought it was so funny to go in and order that. And it was originally just to mess with Jason, showing up at his work, but I think that was one of the first things that made us go, "Oh. This is really fucking good." I've always been interested in how things are made and the effort that goes into things—you taste it in good food.

We grew up so weird in Alaska. My parents were dogsled mushers, so there were points when my family was in a cabin and it was just us, like in a one-room cabin taking baths in a tin trough. On tour I think I force a family vibe a lot of the time because you get so used to your pack and so used to being together. And a bunch of us have construction backgrounds—when you work in construction, you get so used to being with a crew.

So for example, as a band, we always eat with our crew. That's always been the deal since the beginning, and that's something that's really important to us. Something else we started doing a few years ago was—this is a disgusting thing that we do—we started bringing a hot-dog roller on tour. We had stopped into a hardware store and saw that they had a hot-dog roller for customers and thought, "Oh, that's really smart. I can't believe we'd never even thought to look these up!" They're not super expensive, and we ended up getting one that we put backstage with a selection of different sausages and plant-based foods (Alaskans throw everything in the meat grinder). We do it for opening bands, our crew, and house crew.

Which reminds me of something that made a big impact early on. On some of our first opening tours, headliners would cover us at restaurants when we had no money. Circa Survive, Gatsbys American Dream, Minus the Bear—that was this really special thing headliners did for us. It just meant so much, and now we do that as well. So in addition to the band and crew eating together (and the hot-dog roller), if the openers join us at a restaurant, if they're around when we're going to get food, we take care of it.

Opposite top: John Gourley eating backstage at the Hollywood Bowl. Photo by Chantal Anderson.

Opposite bottom: Passing John's uncle's special seasoning to bassist Zachary Carothers. Photo by Chantal Anderson.

REST-STOP: JAPAN

An assortment of onigiri at a Japanese 7-Eleven. Photo by Luke Pyenson.

BY SEN MORIMOTO

The lucky artists who get to perform in Japan often play only one or two shows in Tokyo and/or Osaka. The luckier ones have a handful of dates and get to drive between them. I was one of the luckier ones. Our shows (and meals) in Japan were incredible, but a couple of things stick in my memory above all else: the convenience stores and the rest stops.

My friend Yuki Kikuchi, a photographer based outside Tokyo, was our point person in Japan and plays that role for a lot of indie artists who come over to play shows. I wrote to Yuki—who has several photos in this book—to see if he could photograph some rest stops for us, and he told me he could do even better: He was going on tour with Japanese American jazz-rap ace Sen Morimoto. How about some photos of him on the road?

We followed up with Sen to supplement the visuals with his thoughts on Japanese rest-stop culture. The topic likely won't be entirely unfamiliar to Food People or those who've traveled to Japan, but Sen's perspective as a Japanese American touring musician is both fresh and insightful. *-LP*

The first time I played outside of the States, I was asked to go play a festival in Tokyo, and it was massively impactful. I hadn't thought or expected anything like that would happen or considered how it might feel once it *was* happening. It was so wild. Since then, Japan's become my favorite place to tour.

Both of my parents were born in Japan; my mom is American, but her dad was in the military, and she was born in Kobe. I was born in Japan, too, but we left when I was a baby. I've been going back since I was six for varying amounts of time, mainly because my dad wanted me to speak better Japanese. Now when I come on tour, I can work on my Japanese, I can go visit family, and I can become more connected to that part of myself. It was like a switch flipped when I realized music could allow me to do that.

On trips to visit family in Japan throughout my life, we always took trains. I had never really driven from city to city until I came on tour. That was new for me. Japan has public transit that works for people, and it's actually cheaper and faster than driving. But for tour, driving makes sense—you're bringing your backline with you.

The rest stops in Japan are all so different—they're regionally focused, and the foods on offer are very representative of the specific towns that they're coming from, what they specialize in, and what's in season. It's a really special part of Japanese cuisine in general, and I think it's cool for that to be present even in quick to-go places like rest stops. I feel like the most common thing I hear touring in the US is, "God, I need a vegetable!" But I never feel that way in Japan. You can get anything. You can also

Sen in Japan. Photo by Yuki Kikuchi.

find the most amazing gifts for people, like a special mochi or matcha that's made *only* in that one place.

There are plenty of McDonald's in Japan, but I never see them at rest stops. I just see, like, a fun cake shop, and I'm like, "Who's gonna get cake here? Why are we getting cake?" Literally a wedding cake. But rest stops aren't even just about food—they're like little malls. We stopped at one on the way to Osaka that had a piano store in it. There were full grand pianos at the rest stop, and there was a day-care center next door. It was like, you could drop your kids off, check out the pianos, go get some udon from the noodle shop, and then get back on the road!

The other important thing to talk about is konbini culture. Konbinis are convenience stores, and like so many foreign-language terms in Japan, it got abbreviated [from *konbiniensusutoa*] for the ease of Japanese speakers. There are a few competing top konbinis: 7-Eleven, Lawson, and FamilyMart. 7-Eleven is so different than it is in the States. There's fresh food, there's onigiri, sushi to go, any drink you can think of, incredible snacks, and great coffee, which was new on my fall 2022 tour. Before the pandemic, the most common thing I'd see were the hot cans of coffee in the warming drawer. Now there are self-service coffee machines with fresh-ground beans!

It's a controversial topic, but on that tour I became a FamilyMart guy. It was a discussion I had a lot with Yuki, my tour manager, like, "What's your konbini vibe?" I actually bought FamilyMart socks, and I'm supporting the brand 100 percent now. I just think they have the best selection of grab-and-go foods, and they're partnered with Muji, so they have some fancy Muji snacks (and socks) there too. But I didn't get the Muji-collab socks; I got FamilyMart brand.

I think people in Japan feel similarly about konbini food to how Americans would feel about 7-Eleven pizza, for example. Like, it's full of salt or whatever, and it's not the best for you. I think there is an awareness that it's better than American fast food, but to foreigners visiting Japan, it's really a culture shock to see that fast food there is not "fast food"—it's just food that's prepared quickly, but there's thought and care put into it. But it's funny: I say that to my brother who lives in Kyoto, like, "Yeah, I've been eating at a lot of konbinis, and it's amazing!" and he's like, "Yuck, dude. Cook a meal."

But because of the night-and-day difference between fast food in Japan and the US, I feel so comfortable eating at rest stops and konbinis. Not only is it delicious, but it's really cheap: It's a miraculous win-win. You're like, "Oh my god, this was only five bucks! I got a great meal, I don't feel like shit, and I'm not gonna shit my brains out after this." And if I do, there's a bidet at the 7-Eleven, the seat is heated, and it's singing to you.

A rest stop in Japan. Photo by Yuki Kikuchi.

Green Room Tea

as told by Hicham Bouhasse (Imarhan)

One of the coolest things about our big indie-rock community is its true global scale. Bands from the US are always crossing paths with our British, European, Australian, Kiwi, and South American counterparts, forming friendships and swapping stories. It's also not uncommon, especially on festival bills, to share the stage with groups based out of the Sahara and the Sahel who play a kind of music the Western music press calls "desert blues." One of the best is Imarhan, a Tuareg band from Tamanrasset, Algeria.

I had the chance to see Imarhan at a festival in northern Portugal in 2018—they played right before us on the same stage. Sadly, I was face down on the floor of our green room with food poisoning. I remember hearing their ethereal music in the distance, wishing I could be out there in the crowd. Even so, I was thrilled to be sharing a bill with a band from North Africa.

To say that hospitality is taken seriously in that part of the world is a massive understatement. So I was particularly interested to hear how a band from North Africa experiences life on the road—which can often be so innately inhospitable. I caught up with Imarhan multi-instrumentalist Hicham Bouhasse over a series of WhatsApp voice messages—one of the popular ways that folks communicate in the Sahara—to speak a little about how Imarhan experiences hospitality on tour in a mix of English, French, and Arabic.

When Imarhan came through the US on tour, we were finally going to meet in person and catch up over tea, but extenuating circumstances prevented this from happening multiple times. However, we were able to dispatch Chantal Anderson to photograph the band backstage in LA, and we wanted to share what we could from Hicham, complemented by one of Chantal's wonderful photographs. The warmth from this treasured pre-show ritual practically radiates from the image. *-LP*

First of all, we love the touring life. We've discovered a lot through this journey—different people, different cultures. The most special moments for us are the shows—we enjoy them just as much as the audience. We love what we do. But it can be tiring when we're out for a long time, so the touring life is both a hard and beautiful thing at once. We need to keep a connection with home.

We do have some special dietary needs—we eat only halal meat, and when we don't get that, we become vegetarians! And we actually like to cook for ourselves, when we have time for it. On our rider, we get vegetables, cheese, and fruits like mango, apricot, and pineapple. But we also prepare our tea in the green room— and drink it together, just as we would in Tamanrasset, no matter where we are in the world.

Imarhan backstage at Zebulon in LA, 2022. Photo by Chantal Anderson.

Tasting Uruguay Worldwide

as told by Juan Wauters

Portions translated from the original Spanish by Luke Pyenson

I'm pretty sure that Juan Wauters is a creative genius. He's a prolific artist, and though his work is vast and varied, it's always immediately identifiable. Juan just has a certain "Juan-ness" about his approach to making music that's disarmingly earnest and genuine. It's not unusual for Juan to pack multiple genres into a single song—multiple languages too! I've known him about as long as Real Estate has existed, and he's always been an inspiring character in my scene.

In the early days, we played a few shows together around the country with his first band, the Beets. I can remember sitting on a back porch in Nashville with him and a few other people. Juan was strumming a classical guitar and serenading us all with some Beatles songs. In Juan's hands, even these classic tunes that I've known my whole life somehow sounded new.

It was great to chat with Juan in both English and Spanish about how his upbringing in Uruguay has informed the way he experienced food on tour, particularly in western Europe. At least for us, it was a totally novel—and fascinating—perspective. We'll never gulp down a pre-show Club-Mate in Berlin quite the same way. *–AB*

Where I grew up, in Uruguay, we ate only Uruguayan food. Or, I should say, everything we ate in Uruguay we *thought* was only Uruguayan. This was the pre-internet era; we didn't really know what life was like in other countries, let alone what they ate. The world hadn't been globalized yet, so I didn't know what a taco was, or a pastrami sandwich.

I consider myself Uruguayan because my family's been in Uruguay three generations now, but the history of Uruguay is a little bit complex. The pre-colonization cultures haven't endured and aren't as well known as the Maya or the Incas, for example. We grew up saying we were European, but then I moved to Queens as a teenager, and suddenly I was part of a social group referred to as "Hispanic."

I really don't blame people, but sometimes I hear, "Oh, you're from Uruguay? I've been to Colombia!" Or, "I've been to Mexico!" And I'm like, "Oh, okay!" From where I am right now—Los Angeles—Mexico is maybe two hours away by car. It's twelve hours on a plane from Uruguay.

The most traditional Uruguayan cuisine revolves around meat and fire: the asado. If someone has you over for an asado, it'll be an experience. But other than that, many typical Uruguayan dishes are variations on foods brought by the Italians or the Spanish. I only started to fully realize this when music brought me to those countries on tour.

Years ago, I went to play a show in Genoa, in northern Italy. In Uruguay, we eat a type of spinach pie with egg in it called pascualina. They eat spinach pie in many countries, of course, but in Uruguay that's what we call it. Well, the promoter in Genoa took us out to a meal before the show, and they brought out pascualina. It was very much the same, and they called it the same thing. They were showing it to me with so much pride. I was like, "Oh, I guess this isn't Uruguayan!" To have an Italian guy saying, "This is our traditional Genovese food," it was mind-blowing.

Sometimes people experience the same type of food in completely different ways. I grew up eating Spanish tortilla in Uruguay, which we usually eat with a salad or something. On tour in Spain, I learned that they stuff it in a sandwich! In Uruguay, it's impossible to consider that. Like, you're gonna put tortilla inside bread? It doesn't make any sense. It would be like putting pasta in a sandwich.

But that brings up another story: I was in Paris working on a song with a French producer, and he said, "I'm gonna take you to an Algerian place where they sell these really good sandwiches." In Uruguay, we have a type of chickpea-flour pancake called fainá, which we put on top of pizza (it's called pizza a caballo). At the Algerian place in Paris, that's what they were putting in the sandwiches! A thicker version of fainá called garantita, plus harissa. It was delicious.

Another example is blood sausage. If you'd asked me before I started touring, I'd say it was completely Uruguayan. When I came to the US, I never saw it. But once I started touring, I realized they have it all over the place! I've seen it all throughout Latin America, in Spain, and in the UK, but it's different in every country. In Uruguay, it's just the blood and the fat, no filler.

There are other foods from my childhood I've seen around the world on tour—wheat-shaped pain d'épi in France (we call it pan espiga), or even empanadas, which growing up I didn't realize were eaten all over Latin America. Even drinks have surprised me. It

still cracks me up to hear people order a "cortado" in an American accent. That's common in Uruguay at cafés started by Spanish immigrants in the early twentieth century.

We have a strong coffee culture, but Uruguay is also the maté capital of the world. Seeing Club-Mate in Berlin was interesting, for sure, 'cause at home it's more of a ritual. Everybody sits in a circle, and you share it, you pass it around. We love to sit around and talk, and maté's a big part of that. There are a lot of social codes to it too. Like if you say, "Thank you," that means you don't want to drink any more. Once you say that, the next time around, they skip you. Those things are starting to fade, but they've been a tradition for generations.

One more thing: I remember my neighbor growing up had an avocado tree. Up until I left, it was not a thing to eat avocado at all. Nobody ate it. It was not a part of our diet. Avocados would fall off the tree and rot! When I had one for the first time, I was like, "Oh, wow! This is delicious, actually."

Opposite: Juan in Japan. What is the okonomiyaki reminding him of?
Photo by Yuki Kikuchi.

Shalom Bologna

by Luke Pyenson

As I've grown older, Jewish holidays and their food traditions have become more important to me. Like many secular American Jews of my generation, I can sometimes be facetious or self-deprecating when talking about our culture, but my relationship to Jewishness is more complicated and was always tested the most on tour. Krill was proudly and obviously a band of three Jews, but four-piece Frankie Cosmos had one and a half, and I was the only one consistently missing holidays. One such holiday is the theme of this piece, which happens to take place in a city synonymous with pork. *-LP*

There's something farcical about being a Jew in Bologna on Passover. It may be the very geographical epicenter of trayf, yet its name belies a fair bit of Jewish history, and neighboring Ferrara hosts Italy's most significant Jewish museum. Today the Jewish population is quite small, but it was one stronger the night I played a gig there on Pesach 2019.

Being from the Northeast, as I am, I grew up thinking it's not that uncommon to be Jewish. Touring really changes that. It's amazing. There are other Jews in indie rock, of course, but the *vast* majority of other musicians I've met on the road are not. Even ones who should have been. Stephen Steinbrink! Incredible musician. *Steinbrink*. Not Jewish.

It's hardest on holidays. Tour routings are never designed with Jewish holidays in mind, and to be fair, most secular Jews like me don't know the exact dates of our holidays until a few weeks before. It was always a dance trying to be home for Passover, Rosh Hashanah, and Yom Kippur. I usually managed at least one, but more often than not I found myself in places bereft of Jews, like Salt Lake City or Munich.

Regardless of where I was in the world, the routine would be the same. Do the time-zone math in my head and call in to my family's dinner, where I'd either be put on speaker or passed around the table like a platter of mandelbrot. Each holiday had its attendant foods I longed to be eating: festive round challah on Rosh Hashanah; platters of appetizing, sweet noodle kugel and knishes on Yom Kippur; and, of course, my grandmother's matzo ball soup on Passover.

Fluffy, not quite tennis-ball-sized, and suffused with schmaltz, my grandmother's matzo balls were sensational, made with love and a particular sense of duty that I feel is endemic to the Ashkenazi holiday table. Like, this is the cuisine we got stuck with, so this is what we make. It's good. It's actually very good. But is it a joyful, vibrant cuisine? Maybe sometimes, but definitely not on Passover.

My use of past tense makes it sound like my grandmother's dead, but she isn't—she has Alzheimer's. She no longer cooks, and 2019 was the first year she wouldn't have made matzo ball soup. Even if she had—I was in Bologna. I had already eaten her matzo ball soup for the last time, but I didn't know it, or I hadn't internalized it. I was preoccupied with finding tortellini in brodo before the gig.

Bologna is one of those places we're really lucky to randomly have on the indie-rock circuit. Politically lefty with a big university and a reputation for great food, it's like playing in Berkeley. There's one legendary club—Covo Club—where all the indie bands play, and that's where we were that night. It's a little bit outside the city's medieval core, where golden-hued tortellini fill shop windows.

Despite spending parts of my teens and early twenties making fresh pasta in Italian restaurant kitchens, I had never eaten tortellini in brodo before. While American minds may picture cheese-filled tortellini swimming in red sauce, in Bologna they are filled with three types of pork (prosciutto, mortadella, and pork loin) plus Parmigiano-Reggiano, and served bobbing unceremoniously in cloudy amber chicken broth.

I fantasized, naturally, about eating tortellini in brodo in a casual osteria or trattoria full of locals. Maybe a little spot I stumbled on while walking along Bologna's porticoed side streets or next to the heralded hardware store where I bought bronze pasta tools to bring home. But that's not what happened. Well, I did buy the bronze pasta tools. But for dinner I went to a fast-casual tortellini place and ordered on a touch screen. Between soundcheck and showtime, that's what I had time for.

As anodyne as the restaurant was, my meal didn't disappoint. The delicate tortellini were as fantastic as I'd hoped, but even better was the broth. In fact, a funny thing happened when I took my first bite: I felt like I was at my family's Passover table. Something about the ritual of poking around to trap tortellini, the marriage of rich and austere: It added up.

I had been joking around about being in Bologna on Passover, as I did at the beginning of this piece, but the reality was: It was not an easy day. These types of feelings aren't unique to me, or to Jewish musicians, or to any other musicians for that matter. We all

Top: Lockdown matzo ball soup. Photo by Lauren Martin.

Bottom: The touch-screen tortellini. Photo by Luke Pyenson.

miss holidays, birthdays, weddings, and other significant events, constantly. All the time.

My grandmother's health was slipping away, our family's holidays and their food traditions were changing, and if a torch was being passed, I wasn't even there to receive it. It felt wrong to be off in Italy playing mid-level indie rock to a room of around 150 people. In a way, the unexpected resonance of the tortellini actually made the night harder.

The following Passover—2020—fell during the fourth week of lock-down. I was supposed to be on tour in Australia and New Zealand, but circumstance put me in my childhood kitchen outside Boston rolling matzo balls with my mom for the first time. The store was out of matzo meal, so we ground whole sheets in the food processor. My grandmother was locked down in an assisted living facility about a mile away.

The pandemic reshuffled my priorities. It was one thing to be away from my family on Passover because I was on tour, but the cruelty and irony of Passover 2020 put things into perspective. I was finally home, but we *still* couldn't celebrate all together. In fact, it wasn't until 2022 that my family was able to have a normal holiday. Bands had started to tour again, but we'd just finished a new album and were lying low. I was happy to be home.

A nice ending to this essay could've been: I made tortellini in brodo for my family that year, and it was the best Passover ever. Something like that. But of course I didn't make tortellini in brodo—I'm not a freak! I use my bronze pasta tools from Bologna here and there, but not on Jewish holidays. Torch tacitly passed, I made matzo ball soup, and my grandmother tasted it for the first time. Even though she didn't know and doesn't remember, she loved it.

Golden-Hour Surprise

by Cadien Lake James (Twin Peaks)

It's impossible to imagine getting angry at Cadien Lake James, a guitarist in the versatile rock band Twin Peaks and an absolute staple of the Chicago music scene. Many years ago, I was on a real bummer of a tour in the dead of winter. Attendance was at an all-time low, but when we got to Chicago, Cadien was there with bells on; the show was great. Sometimes all you need is a positive mental attitude to turn things around.

With his jovial smile and overall good vibe, he is the living embodiment of a "big lug." But when you're traveling around the world cramped together in a tiny van for hours on end, it's possible to get sick of almost anybody. Cadien's story is a favorite of mine, and it illustrates that even his bandmates can't stay mad at him for long. *-AB*

I grew up the son of a political-activist-turned-restaurant-owner in Chicago. We lived a block away from my dad's joint, the Heartland Cafe, known as much for its "Good, Wholesome Food for the Mind and Body" as for its importance as a community gathering place. You'd show up to the Heartland Cafe for international music, open mics, or poetry nights; you could also witness political history— it famously hosted events for Harold Washington's successful mayoral bid and Barack Obama's run for the Senate.

It was a safe space and community hub in our little neighborhood of east Rogers Park, and it instilled in me the notion that food is meant to be shared. Even more so, that what we're sharing often goes beyond just food: our stories, our frustrations, our fascinations, our musings, our trials, our love. I ate at least half my meals there until I graduated high school, after which I hit the road for Twin Peaks' first tour. Following that, I did a short stint at Evergreen State College, and then more touring, incessantly, from 2013 until March 2020.

I've been lucky to try a plethora of incredible food and diverse cuisines through my travels playing music. But most of my meals weren't at restaurants as beloved or characterful as the one I grew up in. The great majority of my meals were catered by gas stations:

potato chips, mixed nuts, roller taquitos, sunflower seeds, candy bars, Gatorade. Needless to say, the presence of food as a cultural force, as a spark of community, isn't omnipresent out there on that old white line.

I didn't notice much those first years—too wide-eyed by the excitement of shows, new folks, new states, new countries, cheap shots, and cheap beers to concern myself with sustenance. But as reality set in and the new became the norm, the gorgeous Ritual of the Bard became more demanding, more draining, and more shockingly repetitive. The music and connection with fans are respites—that's the heart—but we aren't meant to squeeze into vans and get truckin' with no time to spare from city to city, all without a chance to soak up the local culture each night.

Oh, to have been in these great cities around the world, but to have not truly seen them!

One thing we do have control over as blue-collar musicians is the Golden Hour: that magic time between soundcheck and the show, the couple-hour stretch where you have nowhere to be and nothing to do. As we got older and better at touring, we realized that the Golden Hour was our opportunity to try the best food we could find in the neighborhood we were playing in. It was also our opportunity to get away from the stresses of the road. Some nights, this little window of time can hold even more weight than the show itself.

I remember one such Golden Hour in Omaha, Nebraska, in 2019. We were having a rough start of tour, overconcerned with ticket sales and attendance upon the release of a new record, and not easily enjoying The Present. The energy was off. I love my bandmates, but that night I needed some time alone, and so did they.

Strolling up the main drag in search of something delicious, I didn't make it far before I was pulled in by the aromas of a hip ramen joint and quickly grabbed a seat at the bar. I was ready to focus on nothing but a big bowl of ramen, conjured from so much labor and so many elements—tender, savory braised chashu; soy-stained, jammy-yolked ajitama; the distilled flavor punch of the tare; the beautiful fatty broth that grips each springy ramen noodle. My food hadn't come yet; ramen just always gets my mouth watering! From anticipation alone, I was transported away.

But the fantasy was short-lived: As I was waiting for my bowl, in came one of my bandmates. Improbably, his quest for a private moment had led him to the same destination, and the only remaining seats surrounded me at the bar.

It sounds made-up, but shortly thereafter, another bandmate strolled in too. Something had brought us together despite an earnest campaign for the opposite, so we sat there in a line, three bandmates with three bowls of ramen, enjoying the absurdity of the moment and the decadent meals before us.

Whether it's coming home to your family to eat together after a long day at work, going out for a bite with a confidant when you need a sympathetic ear, or sitting down with your bandmates after a long drive and a tough soundcheck, sometimes that's all it takes when you have a hard day—taking time to share good company and good food. Even when you didn't mean to.

It's Not about the Pho

by Sebastian Modak (Infinity Girl)

Travel Editor, Off Duty, the *Wall Street Journal*

I first read Sebastian Modak's writing in 2019, when he was the *New York Times* Travel section's "52 Places" traveler, sending dispatches from a different destination each week for the whole year. I was glued to the series, and there was something about the way Seb wrote that I loved but couldn't put my finger on. It wasn't until working on this book that I found out what it was: He's a drummer.

Seb played in the shoegaze band Infinity Girl, which was incidentally part of the same early 2010s Boston scene as my band Krill. His writing has rhythm, and I wasn't surprised at all to learn he used to tour—his nuanced and holistic view of travel and all it entails is clearly the product of someone who hasn't just gone on vacation.

Now the travel editor at the *Wall Street Journal* (following a stint as *Lonely Planet*'s editor at large), Seb was gracious enough to share a memory from his touring days with us. And even though it's not the sunniest piece in the collection, it's just the kind of memory I was hoping for: where food fosters conflict, reveals rifts, and sits at the table quietly simmering, as we ourselves sometimes do. *–LP*

It was quiet, except for the scraping of plastic spoons, the slurping of noodles, and the faint buzz of a fluorescent light dying overhead. Usually, it would be the perfect moment for someone to chime in with a hearty "That's how you can tell the food is good!" But this was not that kind of silence.

We were in Philadelphia, where the night before we had played the last show of a three-week tour. At each stop, we had sweat through our clothes and blown out our eardrums in a different basement or dive bar, from New York, where we were based, into the Midwest, up through Canada, and back along the East Coast. For the four of us that made up Infinity Girl, it was our third or fourth tour ever, and we were all riding high on the novelty of living out a version of our childhood dreams, albeit in a cramped van and on strangers' floors. Until we weren't.

By the morning after that last show, much of the camaraderie and shared joy that had propelled us from show to show seemed to be gone, emulsified like the chicken fat in the bowls of soup we ate in a heavy silence. It was hard to pinpoint exactly what was wrong because so much was. We sat and ate, all of us exhibiting a dangerous blend of sleep deprivation, hangovers, and, in some cases, straight-up anger.

This had been my idea: to have one last meal, a breakfast that had the whiff of adventure to it. It was 2015, and I hadn't yet become a travel writer, a profession that would eventually push music to the sidelines of my life. But I suppose those instincts— to step out of routine and search for a good story when the opportunity arises—were already stirring as I woke up hungry and ready to go looking for a certain mystical chicken pho. Over the years, I had heard whispers of Pho Ga Thanh Thanh, a now-closed soup-slinging outpost on Kensington Ave where the cooks were so confident in their creations that the menu was limited to two options: dark meat or white meat. Despite going to college in Philadelphia, I had never made it there. This was my chance.

Despite being beef pho's less celebrated cousin, sometimes derided by the uninformed as nothing but a cold remedy, a bowl of well-made chicken pho can be a revelation. The broth sparkles with a delicacy that comes from meticulous preparation perfected over generations. Spices need to be proportioned with mathematical precision, and the chicken needs to be soft enough to fall apart with a slight shove of a chopstick, but not so soft that it turns to mush. It took one bite to immediately know Pho Ga Thanh Thanh got it.

I wanted to talk about all of this, to point out that what we were eating was a style of pho ga unique to Vietnam's southern regions, a result of where Philadelphia's (and the country's) Vietnamese diaspora mostly comes from. How that fact, in turn, was a direct reflection of history. Did they know that in Russia and other former Soviet nations, northern recipes are far more common, due to the communist connections between the countries? *Jesus Christ, these noodles were good.* I thought of a dumb joke about *this* being the real chicken soup for the soul and started talking before stopping myself. I could tell from the facial expression on Mitch (bass guitar, childhood best friend, peacemaker) that now was not the right time.

Someone at the table yawned dramatically. Someone else pointed out a hair in his soup, pulling it out slowly, fixing me with a bloodshot stare as he did so. I wondered if anyone had ever been drowned in a bowl of chicken soup before.

The previous evening, the singer of another band on our bill had invited us to stay at his place after the gig, the kind of generous offer we depended on when we were taking home—on a good night—a shared hundred dollars. We didn't expect much from our accommodations, but as we loaded our gear up into the apartment, I could tell this was going to be a particularly rough night's sleep. We unpacked our sleeping bags and prepared to occupy a corner of the small, dusty room. And then the party started.

A few six-packs appeared, and some already-drunk friends of our host arrived. *If you can't beat them . . .* While Mitch and I joined the fray, Nolan (vocals, guitar, introversion) and Kyle (vocals, guitar, long-distance running) tried, impossibly, to sleep. At one point, I glanced over mid-conversation to see Nolan sitting up in a chair, coat still on, arms crossed, beanie pulled down over his face. Kyle was next to him, eyes closed tight, earphones in, listening to one of his soporific podcasts. The polite thing to do would have been to shut the party down for the sake of the sleepy. But this wasn't our apartment, this wasn't our party, and, come on, it was the *last day of tour.*

I don't recall what time things wound down, but I do recall how I felt the next morning. I've never been kicked in the skull by a horse, but I suspect it would be similar to how my head throbbed that morning. My spine felt like it had been taken out piece by piece and rearranged. My lungs were coated with the smoke of a dozen cigarettes. Yes, this absolutely called for a steaming bowl of pho ga.

No one else wanted to make the drive to a seemingly random Vietnamese restaurant that morning. The consensus was to grab a breakfast sandwich as usual and head back home to New York. I was insistent, annoying even. *We have to eat somewhere, so why not make it special? It's the last day of tour; let's celebrate. I will straight-up vomit if I have to eat another shitty convenience-store breakfast sandwich right now.*

So consensus be damned, we went in search of soup. This location of Pho Ga Thanh Thanh was not in a part of town most people would go out of their way to visit on a trip to Philadelphia. Soulless businesses lined a sidewalk where people caught in the dragnet of the national opioid epidemic walked with the staggered steps of TV zombies. Glass from broken car windows blanketed the streets. The tension in the van, already taut as a hand-pulled noodle, intensified. We pulled up to a parking spot, tried our best to cover the thousands of dollars of gear visible through the van windows, and walked to the restaurant.

"How many white meat, how many dark meat?" the server snapped before we had even sat down. I already loved this place. A few moments later, the bowls landed on our table with percussive finality. We dug in. No one else admitted to having the same transcendental experience I did as I felt my mind clear with every sip of broth, trying my best to forensically compile an ingredient list as I ate. *Is that star anise I taste? Cinnamon? How the hell is this chicken so tender?* A lot of people say being in a band is like having another family. Well, if a family thrives on compromise, this time I was the screaming toddler who every once in a while actually gets his way.

In about twenty minutes, all four bowls were, I was relieved to see, drained to their dregs. But only then did the conversations start, and it wasn't the usual careless banter of four friends having the time of their lives. There were complaints about the night before, how we should have shut the party down earlier and insisted on getting some sleep. Someone started moaning about how my pho detour would get us stuck in rush-hour traffic. We started talking about who was going to drive the van all the way back to Boston, where it had to be returned, after dropping us off in New York. Mitch volunteered, though he notably insisted on doing it alone.

A table and a meal can bring people together, but it's just as adept at revealing the cracks between them. At Pho Ga Thanh Thanh, the fissures found in any family started to appear in ours— it was that kind of breakfast-table conversation. This was about wanting to go home, everyone seemed to suggest with every passive-aggressive comment. It was about wanting to sleep. It was about a bowl of pho.

But, of course, it wasn't about those things. Thinking back to the mostly empty restaurant, other moments rise to the surface of my memory as if they are chapters of the same book. Late nights that some in the band wished had ended earlier. Shows not booked, tours not taken. A haziness to the question that is at the heart of any group endeavor: *Why are we doing this?*

When I pushed us to take a little adventure in search of pho, what I was really doing was extending the tour by just a few hours. I may not have realized it, but on some level I knew that this was a period in my life—mid-twenties, professionally adrift, still a little reckless—that wasn't going to last forever. I craved just one more thing. I always do.

Infinity Girl broke up around two years later. Kyle and Nolan, the band's principal songwriters, had decided they weren't having fun anymore after a particularly lackluster show at the Mercury Lounge on New York's Lower East Side. A few weeks later, they shared the news at a restaurant in Bushwick that we'd often stop in before or after shows. There was no mind-bending soup involved, just greasy burgers and cold pints of beer. But it happened around a shared table, and that felt right.

ACKNOWLEDGMENTS

This book wouldn't exist without its dozens of incredible contributors: We can't possibly thank you all enough. We continue to be blown away by the thoughtfulness, creativity, and emotion that went into each and every piece.

We'd like to thank Darryl Norsen for his patience and skill in designing our beautiful cover.

We'd also like to thank the photographers Chantal Anderson, Yuki Kikuchi, Neelam Khan Vela, Pooneh Ghana, and Alissa Anderson for their brilliant images; Lauren Martin for her inspired illustrations; and the many musicians who shared photos from their personal archives.

To Soumeya Bendimerad Roberts, our agent at HG Literary—your belief in our vision gave us the confidence to see it through, and you've helped guide this project with expertise, patience, and unshaking support every step of the way. We're enormously grateful to have you on our team.

To Olivia Roberts, our editor at Chronicle Books—you understood both us and the project from day one (no easy feat) and simply couldn't have been a better fit for this project. We're so grateful to have worked together on this.

To Maggie Edelman, our designer at Chronicle Books—you translated our vague ideas into the beautifully designed book of our dreams. It looks amazing! Thank you.

To Lauren—your incredible illustrations are what everyone can see, but your mark on this book is much bigger than that. Thank you for supporting me at every moment of this process. People like to say it's a bad idea to fall in love with your bandmate, but they couldn't be more wrong.

To my mom, Andrea (my longest writer-editor relationship), and my dad, Eric—thank you doesn't even begin to cover it. I could not have done this—or spent so many years playing music and touring—without your love and support.

To Midge and Jack, origins of my wanderlust and musicianship, respectively—thank you for making all this possible.

Thank you to Craig & Laura, Maxine & Bill, Mickey & Bobbie, David & Loraine, Ian, and all my friends and family. All your support has helped to lift this book up.

To Greta, how was I so lucky to be in your band? And Alex, how was I so lucky to be your bandmate?

And to my Krill bandmates (and successor) Aaron Ratoff, Jonah Furman, and Ian Becker—thank you for being there, via our inane text thread, at all hours of the day, every day. *-LP*

233

To Leanne, who threatened to write this book herself if I wasn't going to—none of this would have happened without you and that first giant push.

To all my bandmates in Real Estate, Taper's Choice, and the Freaks—it's the moments offstage and between the shows that I cherish the most. Thank you for inspiring me and for breaking bread with me after soundcheck.

To Katie Eberle, who believed in us early on, and suffered through a barrage of late-night text messages when we were trying to find the perfect title—we did.

And to my family for their continued support of my creative choices and unconventional career path, thank you. I love you all so much and your value can't be overstated. *-AB*

And lastly, we need to acknowledge a long and incomplete list of folks who left an indelible mark on this project and/or on us along the way. Many thanks to:

John Chavez, Tom Selwyn, Geoff DeVito, Sheryl Julian, Mike "Sipsman" Caulo, Matt Gordy, Kara Zuaro, Tony Kiewel, Nick Duncan, Bekah Zietz Flynn, Clemence Renaut, Suzy Noel, Roxane Dumoulin, David Velemínský, Lukáš Polák, Evan Easthope, Amanda Bartley, Elia Einhorn, BJ Rubin, Jesse Kranzler, Ellis Jones, John Kolodij, Ella Riley-Adams, Mac Cregan, Darius Zelkha, Jordan Kurland, Trey Many, Rich Schaefer, Rich Holtzman, Matt Hanks, Matt Kallman, Mira Kaplan, Justin Danforth, Darl Ferm, Daniel Radin, Tim Cronin, Ben Bernstein, Kevin Kline and Phoebe Cates Kline, Gabriel RiCharde, Tom Rundell, Sean Brook, Adrian McCusker, David Maine, and Gabby Smith.

To all of the musicians we spoke to whose pieces or ideas didn't make it into this book for one reason or another, thank you; these conversations made an impact on us too: Stephin Merritt, Courtney Barnett, Thao Nguyen, Miho Hatori, Naoko Yamano, Joe Kwon, Ryley Walker, Adam Granduciel, Dent May, Lucas Nathan, Rodrigo Amarante, Chuck Inglish, Zac Rae, Dave Depper, Jonathan Snipes, William Hutson, Patrick Hallahan, Dave Longstreth, Azniv Korkejian, Julia Holter, Justin Sullivan, Marc "Brownie" Brownstein, Dave Harrington, and Chris Tomson.

Library of Congress Cataloging-in-Publication Data

Names: Pyenson, Luke, author. | Bleeker, Alex, author.
Title: Taste in Music : Eating on Tour with Indie Musicians / [compiled by]
  Luke Pyenson and Alex Bleeker.
Description: San Francisco, CA : Chronicle Books, 2024.
Identifiers: LCCN 2023052196 | ISBN 9781797224572 (hardcover)
Subjects: LCSH: Concert tours. | Rock musicians--Travel. | Food habits. |
  Caterers and catering.
Classification: LCC ML3534 .T518 2024 | DDC 781.66092/2--dc23/
eng/20231205
LC record available at https://lccn.loc.gov/2023052196

Manufactured in China.

Design by Maggie Edelman.
Illustrations by Lauren Martin.
Cover design by Darryl Norsen.
Case photograph by Neelam Khan Vela.

10 9 8 7 6 5 4 3 2 1

Chronicle Books LLC
680 Second Street
San Francisco, California 94107
www.chroniclebooks.com